MW01029824

PRAISE FOR

THE FAVOR OF GOD

For far too long, people have not recognized God's true desire for His children to be blessed and free from lack in every area of their lives. *The Favor of God* outlines what God's Word has to say on this subject and clearly illustrates how to bring freedom to pass in your life. He challenges the notion of lack and defeat and shows how God's children can lay hold of the principles of His kingdom. You will not only be blessed, but your life will also be changed forever!

Christine Caine
Director of Equip and Empower Ministries and Founder of The A21 Campaign

I have known Jerry Savelle for more than 30 years as a mentor, author and minister. I always refer to him as my "spiritual father"! Jerry has lived his life as a consistent witness to the abundant life of grace and favor that comes with our belief in the goodness and love of our Lord and Savior, Jesus Christ. I highly recommend that everyone read and study *The Favor of God.* This book will be a great encouragement to you as you learn how to live each day expecting the favor of God to be actively operating in your life.

Meadowlark Lemon
Basketball Hall of Famer, Class of 2003

Jerry Savelle has long been one of my favorite ministers and teachers of the Word. His exhortations are filled with a perfect combination of Scripture and real-life examples to aid in stirring our faith and understanding the Word. *The Favor of God* is an excellent example of this balance. Within its pages, he lays out the Scriptural foundation and rock-solid principles of our Christian rights to the unmerited, unending favor of almighty God as it manifests in the favorable treatment that is available in our daily dealings. His real-life examples will stir your faith to believe that you can experience the favor of God in every area of your life—that you, too, can be God's favorite.

Buddy Pilgrim
Minister and Founder of Integrity Leadership
Former President of Pilgrim's Pride Corporation

THE FAVOR *of* GOD

JERRY SAVELLE

For more information and
special offers from Regal Books, email us at
subscribe@regalbooks.com

Published by Regal
From Gospel Light
Ventura, California, U.S.A.
www.regalbooks.com
Printed in the U.S.A.

Library of Congress Cataloging-in-Publication Data
Savelle, Jerry.
The favor of God / Jerry Savelle.
p. cm.
Includes bibliographical references and index.
ISBN 978-0-8307-6413-6 (alk. paper)
1. God (Christianity)—Love. I. Title.
BT140.S28 2012
231′.6—dc23
2012017965

Rights for publishing this book outside the U.S.A. or in non-English languages are administered by Gospel Light Worldwide, an international not-for-profit ministry. For additional information, please visit www.glww.org, email info@glww.org, or write to Gospel Light Worldwide, 1957 Eastman Avenue, Ventura, CA 93003, U.S.A.

To order copies of this book and other Regal products in bulk quantities, please contact us at 1-800-446-7735.

CONTENTS

Foreword 7

Introduction 9

1. Understanding God's Favor 15
2. Getting a Revelation of Favor 35
3. We Have a Heritage of Favor 53
4. Growing in God's Favor 71
5. Moving to a Higher Level of Favor 89
6. Consistent Favor Requires Consistent Obedience 109
7. Positioned for Favor 129
8. Ten Benefits of Walking in God's Favor 149
9. A Designated Time of Favor 169
10. Supernatural Favor for Our Time 187

Appendix: True Stories of the Favor of God 205

FOREWORD

by Kenneth Copeland

I began studying "have faith in God" about 45 years ago, and almost immediately came face-to-face with the grace of God. I found that I could not explore faith without knowing His grace. I'm still studying both!

Anyone who takes to heart, "The just shall live by faith," (Hebrews 10:38) needs to read *The Favor of God* and study it very carefully. The word "grace" means God's favor, presence, influence, help and ability. It is a manifestation of *the blessing* of the Lord. The huge thing about favor and grace, as Brother Savelle develops them in this powerful book, is that God is not holding back His favor. No, just the opposite. Let's look at Scripture to see how God sees faith and grace.

First, in Hebrews 11, we see the great hall of fame of faith. Verse six boldly declares that without faith it is impossible to please Him. Impossible! That's a strong statement. Why, God, is it that You are so demanding that we have faith in You? Why did Jesus command, "Have faith in God" (Mark 11:22)? Romans 4:16 is His answer: "Therefore it is of faith, that it might be by grace; to the end the promise might be sure to all the seed; not to that only which is of the law, but to that also which is of the faith of Abraham; who is the father of us all." God is filled with love for us, desires to favor us and wants to grace us with His presence and awesome power. That's why He demands faith, so that by grace everything He promised can come to pass in our lives. Faith is the victory that overcomes the world. We are world overcomers! His presence, favor, grace and ability all flowing out of His great love for us is that victorious, battle-winning force that nothing in the world order can stand up against.

In over 40 years of ministry, Jerry and Carolyn Savelle have proven out overcoming faith and victory, winning battle after battle, victory on top of victory. God is no respecter of persons. What He has done for the Savelles is available for you and me. Read this book. Really get into it. Then put it to work. Have faith in God so that grace and favor can abound toward you with sufficiency in all things. Favor abounds so you can abound.

Feed on God's faithfulness. This book is favor food (Psalms 37:3-4 and 84:11).

Be blessed.

JESUS IS LORD!

INTRODUCTION

The man seated to my right on the flight to Amsterdam looked at me as if I had a frog on my forehead.

"What in the world are you talking about?" he asked.

After reading an article I didn't agree with on the front page of a national newspaper, I had just declared out loud, "I have the favor of God; therefore, this will not affect me!"

The man must have thought I was speaking to him.

"I'm sorry. I forgot where I was for a moment," I said, hoping my apology would put an end to the conversation before it even got started.

You see, when I'm on my own airplane and I read something I don't like, I just talk back to it. Doing so on a commercial flight is not such a good idea, as I was about to find out.

My fellow passenger persisted. "So tell me, what will not affect you?"

I read him the portion of the article that reported that many of the major nonprofit organizations in America, such as the United Way, the Red Cross, and even several large Christian ministries, had seen their contributions fall steeply as a result of the downturn in the economy. The article went on to say that the current year's financial forecast for nonprofits didn't look good, and the situation wasn't expected to improve anytime soon.

Having listened intently, he asked, "Well, what's that got to do with you?"

"I'm a minister and the founder and president of a nonprofit organization, and I'm decreeing in faith that neither the economy nor this forecast will affect me."

Based on his next question, I could tell that my answer didn't sit well with him.

"What makes you better than them?"

"I'm not saying that I'm any better than them, but I have a covenant with God that entitles me to walk in His favor," I explained. "That's why I'm decreeing that this economic situation will not affect me. My ministry doesn't have to suffer just because other organizations say that the economy is affecting them."

He just glared at me and said, "Whatever." Then he opened his newspaper, raised it up in front of his face, and didn't look at me or say another word for the next eight hours. When we landed in Amsterdam, he stood up, gave me a quick glance, and walked off. Apparently he was still irritated because I wouldn't join the recession and allow someone else's standard to be my standard.

Several days later, while I was ministering and distributing food in Tanzania, I received word from my office back in Fort Worth, Texas, that they had just opened an envelope containing the largest donation the ministry had received all year. Oh, how I wanted to find the guy who had sat next to me on the plane and say just one word to him: "Whatever!"

The Bible says, "For You, O LORD, will bless the righteous; with favor You will surround him as with a shield" (Ps. 5:12). Another translation puts it this way: "You surround them with your favor" (*NIV*). The newspaper reported that the economy was down, and organizations were headed for a tough time, but I can attest that the favor of God surrounded me and the ministry He had entrusted to me. As a rendering of 2 Corinthians 4:1 that I particularly like says, "Therefore, since we do hold and engage in this ministry by the mercy of God [granting us favor, benefits, opportunities, and especially salvation], we do not get discouraged (spiritless and despondent with fear) or become faint with weariness and exhaustion" (*AMP*).

We don't have to be afraid of anything that is going on in the world. As believers, we're surrounded by the favor of God. It goes ahead of us, and it comes behind us. It goes everywhere we go. When the favor of God is on us, opportunities will come our way—opportunities for increase, for promotion, for success and for benefits.

If you're faced with a challenge related to what is happening in society today, tapping into the favor of God will change your situation. Perhaps you're trying to sell a house in a down market, or you want to buy a home but you can't get credit. I've been there, and I'm telling you that the favor of God will change your circumstances. It will open doors for you, and it will even change rules and regulations for your benefit.

In 1997, I wrote a book titled *Walking in Divine Favor*. This book has since gone all over the world. Back in the late '90s, I visited a number of churches that had taken some of the confessions about favor that I'd included in the book and used them when they prayed over their tithes and offerings. At some of the places where I went to speak and minister, I was introduced as "the Favor Man."

If there's one thing my ministry has become most recognized for over the past decades, it's the teaching and preaching about

God's favor. I've taught people all over the world the importance of declaring God's favor out loud on a consistent basis. It's not enough simply to think about God's favor; the way we tap into it is by declaring it out loud—just like I did on that airplane.

Now, you would think that with so much recognition and so many opportunities to teach about the favor of God, the Favor Man himself would never allow his application of such a significant revelation to fall by the wayside. But that's exactly what happened to me. I didn't do it consciously, but at some point I stopped being consistent with my confession. I thought a lot about the favor of God, but I was not declaring it as I once had done. As a result, the victories I experienced were not as consistent as they had been in the past, and my battles of faith lasted a lot longer than they should have.

When I sought the Lord about this, He reminded me that I had let the revelation of His favor fade from the forefront of my attention and practice. He said, "You're not declaring My favor on your life as consistently as you once did, and consequently, you're not experiencing as many extraordinary things happening in your life."

Notice that God didn't tell me I needed some new revelation that nobody had ever heard. Instead, He pointed me back to a truth He had already revealed to me—one that I had let slip. The apostle Paul said, "We ought to give the more earnest heed to the things which we have heard, lest at any time we should let them slip" (Heb. 2:1, *KJV*). In modern-day vernacular, Paul is saying that we need to get back to the basics.

Imagine the coach of a once-proud professional football team that started a season with four losses and no wins taking his team to the locker room and saying, "Gentlemen, I've discovered what's missing; I know why we're losing. We need to come up with a play that nobody's ever seen before." You and I both know that's not what it's going to take to make that team a winner again. I'll tell you what the coach is going to do. He's going to take his team to the locker room, pull out the chalkboard, and point his players back to the basics.

I recently watched a documentary about Vince Lombardi, the famous coach of the Green Bay Packers who led his team to back-to-back league championships and two Super Bowl victories. Lombardi never had a losing season as a head coach in the NFL, perhaps, in part, because he began each new season by holding up the football and saying to his team, "Gentlemen, this is a football." In doing so, he was preventing his players from ever assuming that the basics were not relevant. It didn't matter that these seasoned athletes had won the Super Bowl; Lombardi still always started with the most fundamental truth about the game: "Gentlemen, this is a football." Then he went on to the *X*s and *O*s—to blocking, tackling, passing and receiving—making the players go through these essentials over and over again.

He told them, "I know I can't reach perfection, but you will learn how to strive forth like never before under my leadership. And as a result, we will get as close to perfection as we can." Lombardi's insistence on sticking with the basics enabled him to achieve a winning percentage of almost 74 percent in the regular season and an astounding 90 percent in the postseason.

As impressive as these statistics are, his success on the field is not Lombardi's greatest legacy. At his funeral, one of his former players eulogized him with these words: "He not only taught us how to win at football; he taught us how to be winners in life."

In Psalm 30:5, we read that God's favor "is for life." God wants us to be winners throughout our entire lives, which is why He has given us His favor. As believers, this lifetime of favor is one of our biggest assets, but we'll never achieve the victories God has in store for us if we don't tap into that favor.

My purpose in writing this book is to help you take hold of the favor of God that is already yours. We'll begin by laying a basic foundation concerning the heritage of favor that is ours as believers. Next, we'll learn how becoming favor-minded and being consistently obedient to speak the Word of God in faith will move us to a fuller experience of favor in our everyday lives. We'll study 10 specific benefits of God's favor as outlined in the Bible, and I'll share personal stories of God's favor in operation in my own life.

Some who read this book will be going back to the basics by revisiting the revelation they received years ago, just like I did. Others will be hearing these truths for the first time. Regardless of whether you are a seasoned believer or a newcomer to the revelation of the favor of God, I can promise you one thing: You are about to experience the favor of God operating in your life like never before.

I invite you now to join me on a journey of faith as together we tap into the favor of God.

I

UNDERSTANDING GOD'S FAVOR

If there's one thing that has blessed me more than anything else over my 40 years of ministry, it's the revelation I've received about walking in the favor of God.

I've come to understand that when I consistently declare the favor of God over my life, extraordinary things happen. I'm not talking about an occasional surprising occurrence; I mean that extraordinary things happen on almost a daily basis.

I have seen the favor of God open doors for me that no man could shut. I have received preferential treatment in matters ranging from the mundane to the astonishing. I have witnessed God's favor change rules, regulations and policies, when necessary, to get me exactly where God wanted me to be. Having seen the favor of God work so powerfully in my own life, I can assure you that it will bring you through even the toughest times and the most overwhelming of circumstances.

The *New King James Bible* identifies Psalm 102 as "a Prayer of the afflicted, when he is overwhelmed and pours out his complaint before the LORD." The psalmist begins, "Hear my prayer, O

LORD, and let my cry come to You. Do not hide Your face from me in the day of my trouble; incline Your ear to me; in the day that I call, answer me speedily" (vv. 1-2). He gets right to the point with God, doesn't he? To paraphrase, he's saying, "God, I need an answer fast. Don't talk to me about being patient; I need to hear from you, and I need to hear from you now."

The psalmist goes on to say,

> For my days are consumed like smoke,
> and my bones are burned like a hearth.
> My heart is stricken and withered like grass,
> so that I forget to eat my bread.
> Because of the sound of my groaning
> my bones cling to my skin.
> I am like a pelican of the wilderness;
> I am like an owl of the desert.
> I lie awake,
> and am like a sparrow alone on the housetop.
> My enemies reproach me all day long;
> those who deride me swear an oath against me
> (Ps. 102:3-8).

This man was in a situation where not only were his enemies coming against him, but other people were also mad at him. Things had gotten so bad that he was unable to make it through the day without weeping. The trial he was going through was so consuming that it stayed on his mind 24 hours a day.

Oftentimes when we're in the midst of a trial, the problem we're facing becomes so overwhelming that we forget our covenant with God. As a result, we become problem-minded rather than being solution-minded. The psalmist apparently struggled with this same tendency:

> For I have eaten ashes like bread,
> and mingled my drink with weeping,
> because of Your indignation and Your wrath;
> for You have lifted me up and cast me away.
> My days are like a shadow that lengthens,
> and I wither away like grass.
>
> But You, O LORD, shall endure forever,
> and the remembrance of Your name to all generations.
> You will arise and have mercy on Zion;
> for the time to favor her,
> yes, the set time, has come (Ps. 102:9-13).

Notice that although this man was initially overwhelmed by his adversity, in the midst of his cry to God he remembered that he was entitled to God's favor. The reason he knew he was entitled to favor is that he was a covenant man, and in declaring that the set time for God's favor had arrived, he became a solution-minded covenant man.

When we choose to enter into covenant with God, we no longer have to fight our own battles; His favor will enable us to attain victory over every situation and circumstance. We see this truth powerfully articulated in Psalm 44:3: "For they did not gain possession of the land by their own sword, nor did their own arm save them; but it was Your right hand, Your arm, and the light of Your countenance, because You favored them."

WHEN WE CHOOSE TO ENTER INTO COVENANT WITH GOD, HIS FAVOR WILL ENABLE US TO ATTAIN VICTORY OVER EVERY SITUATION AND CIRCUMSTANCE.

God's people did not experience victory because of their own might, their own strength, or their own power. The land for which they had believed—the land that had been promised to them by God—became theirs because of God's favor.

I'm not saying that just because we are in covenant with God, we will never have to fight a battle of faith. I'm not a novice: I know how to believe God, I know how to walk in faith, and I know how to overcome adversities. Yet there have been times when I've been through lengthy battles that I should have won long before I did. My problem was that I had let the revelation of God's favor slip. Others who find themselves engaged in long-term struggles may simply not yet have received this revelation.

Often, when the battle is long, and people do not see their prayers being answered when and how they want them to be answered, they blame God. I've been asked, "Brother Jerry, why isn't God listening to me? Why isn't He doing something? What's the problem?"

My answer is always, "God is not the problem. The problem is a lack of understanding." Most of the time, the reason we experience delays in our prayers being answered is that we do not have a right understanding of the favor of God. Without an understanding of the favor of God, we will not appropriate it and confess it on a consistent basis.

What Is the Favor of God?

In order to understand the favor of God, we first need to know the meaning of the word "favor." The term has four main definitions.

Definition #1: Something Granted Out of Goodwill

In other words, the favor of God is granted out of His goodwill toward us. It's not something that can be bought, and it's not something that can be earned. In the most profound demonstration of this kind of favor, Jesus willingly went to the cross in our behalf—not because we deserved to be saved, but because God chose to show us mercy (see Rom. 5:8). Because of the price Christ paid, we are now entitled to walk in God's favor from day to day. Many times, this kind of favor is manifested through God giving us the desires of our hearts.

For instance, I have always loved baseball. I love to play it and I love to watch it. As a kid growing up in Louisiana in the 1950s, my favorite team was the New York Yankees. My favorite player was Mickey Mantle; he was my idol. My glove had to be a Mickey Mantle signature glove, my Louisville Slugger had to have Mickey Mantle's name on it, and my baseball uniform had to be number 7. I'm telling you, I loved Mickey Mantle.

I remember sitting with my dad in front of our black-and-white television, eating popcorn and watching the Yankees. Now and then, there would be a shot of the people in the stands, and I remember one particular time when I saw a little boy about my age sitting there in Yankee Stadium wearing his Yankee cap. I thought he had to be the luckiest kid in the world, because he got to watch Mickey Mantle knock the ball over the fence. Left-handed, right-handed—it didn't make any difference; Mickey could hit them out of the park either way. Then there were Roger Maris, Whitey Ford, and, of course, Yogi Berra. Oh, how I dreamed of going to New York to watch the Yankees play! But for many years, it seemed like this Louisiana boy's dream would never come true.

Decades later, in the summer of 1994, I was in Canada prior to attending a scheduled meeting in New Jersey. I had a couple of free days before I was to preach, so I flew into New York City to spend time with some friends at their home. After having dinner together Friday evening, they asked if there was anything I would like to do the following day.

"Yes," I said, "I want to go see the Yankees play." Then I told them about my childhood dream of seeing Mickey Mantle in person at Yankee Stadium. Of course, by then Mickey Mantle was no longer playing ball, but I still wanted to watch the Yankees play.

"I don't even know if they are playing tomorrow," my friend told me. "They may be on the road, but I'll go check and see."

A short time later, while I was in the guest room unpacking my bag, I heard the sound of someone running in the hall; after a few more seconds, my friend and his wife appeared at the door. "Brother Jerry," he said, "you beat anything we've ever seen."

"What do you mean?" I asked.

He explained that he had just called a man he worked with—a Yankee fan whose season tickets were on the front row of the box seats located right over third base. "The Yankees are in town tomorrow, and my co-worker wants you to be his guest for the game."

I smiled to myself as I thought about the favor of God. But then my friend added, "And guess what? It's Old-Timers' Day, and Mickey Mantle is going to be there!"

I went to sleep that night thinking about the goodness of God and thanking Him for getting me a ticket to see Mickey Mantle in Yankee Stadium.

The next day, as I sat in the box over third base with my Yankee cap on my head, it was 1957 again and I was that little boy at Yankee Stadium. So many of the old-timers I grew up watching on television were there in person: Joe DiMaggio, Whitey Ford, and my own hero, Mickey Mantle. It was a day I will never forget, because it was a day on which God favored me with His goodwill and fulfilled a deep-seated desire of my heart.

But this story doesn't end with my watching the Yankees play and getting to see the old-timers. Mickey Mantle was living in Dallas, Texas, at that time, and about a month later, on a flight to Detroit, we wound up sitting right next to each other.

Some people have said that was just a coincidence, but I call it favor. The Word of God says, "Trust in the LORD, and do good; dwell in the land, and feed on His faithfulness. Delight yourself also in the LORD, and He shall give you the desires of your heart" (Ps. 37:3-4).

When we feed on God's faithfulness and favor, it is only natural that the desires of our hearts will be fulfilled—including those desires we have held close since childhood.

Definition #2:
A Gift Bestowed as a Token of Regard, Love or Friendliness

Have you ever asked someone, "Would you do a favor for me?" What you're actually asking is: "Would you bestow a gift or a token of our friendship?" That's what a favor is—a token of friendship.

Not too long ago, a Christian businessman who also happens to be a friend of mine approached me after a worship service. He said, "Brother Jerry, I really need for you to pray over my business. It's falling apart, and to be honest with you, without God's supernatural intervention, I'm going to lose it."

I had known this man for a number of years. He was a tither in his church, and he supported a number of ministries. He went on to tell me that it wasn't just his business that was at stake; his home and all of his personal property were also at risk.

"Brother Jerry, I know that God gave me this business, and He has blessed me and my family through it. This is an all-out attack of the devil."

When my friend said that, the compassion of the Lord Jesus began to rise up in me. I took his hand and heard myself pray in an unexpected way. I said, "Lord Jesus, as a favor to me, intervene for my friend."

I can't think of a time I had ever prayed like that before. I usually begin my prayers with "Father, in the name of Jesus," and then I quote the Word—but not this time. All I did was ask the Lord Jesus to do something as a favor to me.

Three days later, I got a call from my friend. When I answered the phone, he exclaimed, "Man, I'm telling you, I don't know what you did or said, but God came through with a supernatural breakthrough!"

When I asked the Lord why He had moved so quickly in behalf of my friend, He said, "Because you asked me for a favor."

Then I asked Him, "Do I really carry that much weight with You?"

"You don't realize it, but you have that kind of favor with Me. Wouldn't you do the same for Me if I came to you and said, 'Jerry, I need a favor'?"

ANY TIME WE ARE DEALING WITH FAVOR, WE ARE ACTUALLY FINDING OUT HOW STRONG THE RELATIONSHIP IS.

That's when I realized that any time we are dealing with favor—whether with God or with fellow human beings—we are actually finding out how strong the relationship is. When one of my daughters comes to me and asks for a favor, it really gets my attention and draws on my compassion. If I have the means and the power to do what is asked, I will do it—as a token of my love for my daughter.

Jesus said, "And whatever you ask in My name, that I will do, that the Father may be glorified in the Son. If you ask anything in My name, I will do it" (John 14:13-14). In other words, Jesus is saying, "Our relationship is so strong that if you ask Me to do anything that will bring glory to My Father, I will do it."

Learning this powerful truth about God's favor and the strength of my relationship with Him has changed my prayer life, and it will change yours as well. We can walk in the assurance that "the LORD will give grace [favor] and glory; no good thing will He withhold from those who walk uprightly" (Ps. 84:11).

DEFINITION #3:
PREFERENTIAL TREATMENT

We've already discussed the fact that we have the favor of God; according to His Word, we also have favor with man: "But let your heart keep my commands; for length of days and long life and peace they will add to you. "Let not mercy and truth forsake you; bind them around your neck, write them on the tablet of your heart, and so find favor and high esteem in the sight of God and man" (Prov. 3:1-4).

I have found that when I consistently declare God's favor over my life, I receive preferential treatment from all kinds of people.

When I was in high school, I loved working on cars; my ambition was to own my own business and spend the rest of my life on a racetrack somewhere. I also dreamed of going to the Indianapolis 500, but that was another youthful longing that went unfulfilled–until several years ago.

I got a call from a friend of mine who is a deputy sheriff in Marion County, Indiana. He was planning a special meeting for people who lived in Indianapolis's inner-city housing projects–an area struggling with high rates of crime, drug use and prostitution–and he wanted me to participate in the gathering. Of course, I agreed to go, and as it turned out, we had a great meeting.

Afterward, my friend said, "Brother Jerry, I want you to come with me to the sheriff's office, because there's something we want to do for you." So we got into his cruiser and off we went; I had no idea what they had planned, but it was fun getting to ride in the patrol car.

When we entered the building, I was asked to go into a small room and stand in a certain spot so that they could take my picture. Then my friend told me to wait for a few minutes, and he would be right back. I thought, *Dear God, what have I done?*

In a little while, my friend came back to get me. He escorted me to a room where the sheriff and several other high-ranking members of the department were waiting. To my surprise, they presented me with a photo ID card (featuring the "mug shot" they had taken earlier) and a badge. The sheriff said, "We just want you to know how much we appreciate your coming here and helping us in the inner city. As a token of our appreciation, you are now an honorary deputy sheriff in Marion County, Indiana."

I breathed a sigh of relief that I was not under arrest, and then I thanked him.

"We want you to understand that the title of honorary deputy sheriff entitles you to certain privileges," the sheriff explained. "Is there any place in Indianapolis that you would like to go?"

Without hesitating, I said, "Yes, sir, there's something I've been wanting to attend since I was a kid—the Indianapolis 500."

The sheriff said, "Well, we can make that happen. We'll pick you up in a squad car and take you right into the gate; you won't have to fight the crowd. Just show your badge and you can get into anything you want to get in."

I would have been totally happy just being in the stands somewhere and hearing the roar of engines, but God does exceedingly abundantly above all we can ask or think.

The following Memorial Day, just as they had promised, they picked me up in a squad car and drove me to the Indy. With more than half a million people already there, the crowd was pretty intimidating. But the sheriff drove me right up to the gate leading to the garages, where the cars and drivers were.

I stepped out of that squad car, walked up to the gate, and showed the guard my badge. He let me through the gate, and I went straight to the garages, where I got to meet the drivers and watch their teams tune the engines before the race. But there's more. I didn't get to go to the Indy just once; I've been many times since that first race I attended. I have met the drivers, I've been allowed to sit in the cars, and I've been right there with them up until a few minutes before hearing those famous words: "Gentlemen, start your engines."

Two very special photos taken at the Indy hang in my office: One shows me putting fuel in Mario Andretti's car, and in the other, I am shaking hands with A.J. Foyt. Each time I look at those photos, I am reminded of how the favor of God produces preferential treatment for those who love the Lord.

DEFINITION #4:
ADVANTAGE

Having an advantage means having something working for us that others do not have working for them. For believers, that something is the favor of God.

When my wife, Carolyn, and I bought our first home in Fort Worth, we experienced just this kind of favor. It was 1974, and we had been renting a house while I worked as an associate minister for Kenneth Copeland prior to launching out into our own ministry.

Before we moved to Fort Worth to work for Brother Copeland, Carolyn and I had owned several homes in Shreveport. We had good credit and funds from the sale of our last house available for a nice down payment, but as far as a lender was concerned, launching a ministry was the same as starting a business, which meant we didn't qualify for a home loan.

We had learned how to live by faith, and we knew God would meet all of our financial needs. But the mortgage company wanted something more specific regarding where our support would be coming from. They also said we would need a co-signer. In other words, they were probably not going to loan us the money.

Carolyn and I had found the house that we knew God wanted us to have, and we informed our realtor that despite what the mortgage company said, the house would be ours. When he called a few days later to tell us that the seller had accepted a contract from a couple that was qualified for financing, I told him, "I am not moved by what I hear." He asked what on earth I was talking about, and I told him that according to Mark 11:23, I could have whatever I said, and I was saying that the house was going to be mine. I'm pretty sure he had never worked with a client quite like me.

Even though there was a contract on the house, and the other couple was well qualified, Carolyn and I continued to believe that somehow it would be ours. We would drive by the house and talk about what a wonderful time we were going to have raising our kids there. If our realtor had known we were doing this, I'm sure he would have thought we were nuts.

Then, just a few days before the other couple was scheduled to close on the house, our realtor called again. "Mr. Savelle, I don't understand what just happened, but the other couple has decided not to take the house. All I know is that they said they felt like it wasn't meant to be theirs. I don't know what you and your wife have been doing or saying, but apparently this really is your house."

"I've been trying to tell you that for two months," I said. "The lease is up in two weeks on the place where we've been living; you and the mortgage company need to get to work on our new place."

The day before we had to be out of our rental house, I called the realtor to let him know we were prepared to move into the new house the following day. He said, "You can't move into that house. You don't have loan approval, nothing's been signed, and it's not yours."

"Well, Carolyn and I believe that we'll be moving out of here and into that house tomorrow," I said, "so you'd better get busy."

Later that evening he called again. "I've never seen anything like this in my life," he told me. "I just got the owner's approval for you to go ahead and move in tomorrow."

That's just what Carolyn and I did, and we didn't give another thought to the paperwork or the mortgage company's requirements or what anyone told us we could or could not do where buying that house was concerned. We knew that was the house God wanted us to be in, which meant we had the advantage.

I want you to know that God changed all the rules and all the policies, and we finally bought that house. We worked on it, and

Carolyn did such a good job putting her touch on it that some people came along about four years later and fell in love with the place. They decided they just had to have it, so we sold it to them and doubled our investment.

When we have the favor of God on our lives, we've got an advantage. We've got something on us, around us and with us that others don't have. Life gets more and more exciting every day when we understand that we have the favor of God, because we begin to expect it everywhere we go.

God's Purpose for Bestowing Favor

We know that everything God does for us is motivated by His deep and abiding love for mankind, as this familiar verse tells us: "For God so loved the world that He gave His only begotten Son, that whoever believes in Him should not perish but have everlasting life" (John 3:16). Through the sacrificial blood of God's own Son, Jesus, we have been redeemed–and through our faith in Jesus, we are eligible to inherit every promise God has made in His Word.

Let's take a look at some of the earliest promises of God recorded in the Word and see what His favor is intended to produce in the lives of those who obey Him:

> Now it shall come to pass, if you diligently obey the voice of the LORD your God, to observe carefully all His commandments which I command you today, that the LORD your God will set you high above all nations of the earth. And all these blessings shall come upon you and overtake you, because you obey the voice of the LORD your God:

Blessed shall you be in the city, and blessed shall you be in the country.

Blessed shall be the fruit of your body, the produce of your ground and the increase of your herds, the increase of your cattle and the offspring of your flocks.

Blessed shall be your basket and your kneading bowl.

Blessed shall you be when you come in, and blessed shall you be when you go out.

The LORD will cause your enemies who rise against you to be defeated before your face; they shall come out against you one way and flee before you seven ways.

The LORD will command the blessing on you in your storehouses and in all to which you set your hand, and He will bless you in the land which the LORD your God is giving you.

The LORD will establish you as a holy people to Himself, just as He has sworn to you, if you keep the commandments of the LORD your God and walk in His ways. Then all peoples of the earth shall see that you are called by the name of the LORD, and they shall be afraid of you. And the LORD will grant you plenty of goods, in the fruit of your body, in the increase of your livestock, and in the produce of your ground, in the land of which the LORD swore to your fathers to give you. The LORD will open to you His good treasure, the heavens, to give the rain to your land in its season, and to bless all the work of your hand. You shall lend to many nations, but you shall not borrow. And the LORD will make you the head and not the tail; you shall be above only, and not beneath, if you heed the commandments of the LORD your

> God, which I command you today, and are careful to observe them (Deut. 28:1-13).

God's purpose in bestowing favor hasn't changed since Moses spoke these words many centuries ago. God bestows favor for our success. He wanted His people to be successful then, and He wants us to be successful now.

GOD BESTOWS FAVOR FOR OUR SUCCESS. IT MAKES HIM LOOK GOOD—PARTICULARLY WHEN WE ATTRIBUTE OUR SUCCESS TO HIM.

God has a motive for wanting us to be successful: It makes Him look good—particularly when we attribute our success to Him. When someone asks, "How did you get that promotion?" or "How did you become the salesperson of the year when you don't have nearly as much expertise as some of the other people in this company?" we have an opportunity to tell them about the favor God has shown us—and wants to show them.

God's favor on a person's life is there for the primary purpose of bringing the person success so that God will become attractive to somebody else. We just read, "Then all peoples of the earth shall see that you are called by the name of the LORD" (Deut. 28:10). The passage goes on to say where this will happen: "in the land of which the LORD swore to your fathers to give you" (v. 11).

So, we see that not only does the favor of God on our lives bring Him glory and honor, but it also enables us to take possession of the things God has promised in His Word. Remember what we read earlier in Psalm 44:3: "For they did not gain possession of the land by their own sword, nor did their own arm save them; but it was Your right hand, Your arm, and the light of Your countenance, because You favored them."

The favor of God on our lives enables us to do what we cannot do on our own; it enables us to do supernatural things. We could say that the favor of God is what causes God's "super" to be added to our "natural"—and as a result, the supernatural takes place. As I've discovered over the years, that favor can produce what money can't buy.

I could not accomplish all that God has called me to do, both in the United States and around the world, without an airplane. I'm happy to report that over the course of the past 40 years, our ministry has owned several airplanes—and on more than one occasion, God has used those planes to teach me (and others) valuable lessons about His favor and provision.

At one point, I was believing God for a particular jet that cost $1.5 million. Someone who was part of our ministry at the time asked, "How in the world do you ever expect to get that jet, when you don't even have $100 in the aviation account?"

Welcome to the ministry, I thought. Truth be told, I've never had the money in the account when God told me to do something. Not one time has God ever instructed me to do this or that—to build something, or to stretch and expand the ministry in some fashion—and then asked me, "By the way, Jerry, how much money do you have?" When God instructs me to do something, I know the money will come; my job is to believe Him for it.

I turned to the individual who had asked how I expected to get the jet and said, "I'll get that jet the same way I got every other airplane this ministry has ever owned: I'll sow and reap."

I've only ever bought one airplane in this ministry; the others have been given to me. And the one I bought was my fault. I thought it was taking God too long to get it to me, so I decided to help Him out.

I had received a call from a man who told me he had an airplane he thought I should have, and he was willing to let me have it at wholesale. He invited me to meet him at Meacham Field in Fort Worth so that we could talk about it.

I was desperate for an airplane at that time, so I jumped at the opportunity. When I got to Meacham Field and saw the plane, I thought, *Oh yeah, this is the one; and for the price he's asking, it just has to be God.* Never mind that God had already told me He never wanted me flying an airplane that had debt on it.

Despite the fact that I didn't have the funds on hand to pay for that plane, I agreed to buy it—and I borrowed the money. My reasoning was, *God is taking too long. I need it now, and I can believe for the money after I get the airplane.* Besides, I figured the note wouldn't be all that much, because the price of the airplane wasn't all that much.

I got the airplane, and for the entire time I owned it, making that monthly payment was the hardest thing I'd ever done. One day I asked the Lord, "Why aren't You helping me here?"

He said, "You produced this Ishmael. I didn't."

"Well, what can I do about it?"

"If you'll believe Me to pay it off, and if you'll sow it and give it away, I'll bless you with the airplane I want you to have."

I said, "If I can believe for the money to pay it off, then I'll just keep it, thank You."

"No, it won't work that way," He said.

I decided that if I wanted to get out of the mess I'd gotten myself into, I'd best do exactly as God said. When we take matters into our own hands, as Abraham once did, we almost always get into trouble. Anything born of the flesh as the result of our own scheming is an Ishmael; Isaacs are born of the Spirit according to God's design (see Gen. 16–17). That airplane was an Ishmael to me.

Once I believed God for the money to pay it off so that I could then give it away, the funds came quickly. When I asked the Lord what He wanted me to do with it, He told me to give it to Happy Caldwell, the pastor of Agape Church in Little Rock, Arkansas. That's exactly what I did, and that plane turned out to be a blessing to him. It had been an Ishmael to me, but it was an Isaac to Happy.

As I mentioned before, that was the only airplane this ministry has ever purchased. Every other one has been given to us—including the $1.5 million jet that God did, in fact, supply.

The favor of God on our lives brings about things that seem impossible from a human perspective—and it guarantees victory, no matter how much our adversaries oppose us. I love the Scripture verse that says, "By this I know that thou favourest me, because mine enemy doth not triumph over me" (Ps. 41:11 *KJV*). When we are consistently declaring and walking in the favor of God, it is impossible for the enemy to prevent us from succeeding in the things that God has called us to do.

2

GETTING A REVELATION OF FAVOR

My grandson, Mark James, once accompanied me on a trip to London. When we got to the Dallas-Fort Worth Airport on a Sunday afternoon, the place was a madhouse. The long line leading to the check-in counter snaked its way through row after row of roped stanchions. As if that line—which extended all the way to the entry door of the terminal—wasn't bad enough, once travelers made it through check-in, they had to go through the security line, which was even longer.

We had arrived the required two hours before an international flight, but my experience flying all over the world told me that it would take us at least an hour to check in and then another hour to get through security—plus the time it would take to walk to our gate. Humanly speaking, there was a good chance we were going to miss that flight—but I knew there was more to the picture than what we saw in front of us.

I had been confessing the favor of God over our journey since we'd left the house, and I fully expected that I would now experience that favor at the airport. "Mark James," I said as we stepped into line, "you just stand right here with the luggage for a moment; I'm going to walk up there to the counter and see if my executive travel card will help us with this process."

I held my British Air Travel Club card in front of me as I walked toward the front of the line—and before I even got to the counter, one of the employees said, "Sir, come over here, please; I can take care of you."

I called for Mark James to bring the luggage, and we got right through that line—and the next one. On the way to our gate, I smiled, looked at my grandson, and said, "Now that's the favor of God."

The Lord had spoken to me a number of years before, instructing me that every time I experienced the favor of God, I was to say it out loud right then. He explained that the more I became aware and expectant of His favor, giving Him praise for it the moment I experienced it, the more His favor would manifest. I have found this to be true in situations both large and small—including things like finding a front-row parking spot at a heavily congested shopping mall. God appreciates people who demonstrate an attitude of gratitude. I can assure you that those who are grateful for what God has done for them will see more of the favor of God on their lives.

Mark James and I experienced the favor of God in a variety of situations while we were in England. Each time, I declared, "That's the favor of God, son! We have favor with God and with man." It wasn't long before he began saying it, too: "Papa, that was the favor of God, wasn't it?"

I was thrilled to watch my grandson get his own revelation of the favor of God on that trip, just as I have been privileged to witness many others do throughout the years I've been teaching about God's favor. Getting a revelation of the favor of God is a powerful and transformative experience; it has the potential to change every negative circumstance and situation that a person faces.

It is important to note that the revelation of God's favor comes first through a revelation of Jesus Christ. The Word of God says, "Therefore gird up the loins of your mind, be sober, and rest your hope fully upon the grace that is to be brought to you at the revelation of Jesus Christ" (1 Pet. 1:13). The *Amplified* version of this verse says, "Set your hope wholly . . . on the grace (divine favor) that is coming to you."

Notice that the *New King James* text uses the word "grace," which the *Amplified* translates as "divine favor." The Hebrew word for grace is *chen*, which is defined as "favor, kindness and graciousness." When we translate *chen* as "divine favor," Scripture takes on a whole new meaning. Try it for yourself: As you read and study God's Word, anytime you see the word "grace," stop and translate it as "divine favor," and then take some time to meditate on that verse. Doing so will change your life as you discover that the revelation of God's favor always produces blessing.

Moses understood the connection between favor and blessing. Before he died, he blessed each of the tribes of Israel, making the following declaration over Naphtali: "O Naphtali, satisfied with favor, and full of the blessing of the LORD, possess the west and the south" (Deut. 33:23). Notice the connection between favor and the blessing of God, which ultimately enabled the tribe of Naphtali to possess the land that was to be theirs.

God's favor on a person's life will produce blessing. What's more, God gets great pleasure out of being able to demonstrate His favor in our behalf: "Let them shout for joy and be glad, who favor my righteous cause; and let them say continually, 'Let the LORD be magnified, who has pleasure in the prosperity of His servant' " (Ps. 35:27).

GOD'S FAVOR WILL PRODUCE BLESSING. HE GETS GREAT PLEASURE OUT OF BEING ABLE TO DEMONSTRATE HIS FAVOR IN OUR BEHALF.

As we take the time to translate the word "grace" as "divine favor" and to meditate on what the Word is saying to us, we will begin to experience the continuous blessing that the revelation of God's favor brings into our lives. One person who experienced such a revelation was the apostle Paul. Consider what he wrote in his letter to the Corinthians:

> And lest I should be exalted above measure by the abundance of the revelations, a thorn in the flesh was given to me, a messenger of Satan to buffet me, lest I be exalted above measure. Concerning this thing I pleaded with the Lord three times that it might depart from me. And He

> said to me, "My grace is sufficient for you, for My strength is made perfect in weakness." Therefore most gladly I will rather boast in my infirmities, that the power of Christ may rest upon me. Therefore I take pleasure in infirmities, in reproaches, in needs, in persecutions, in distresses, for Christ's sake. For when I am weak, then I am strong (2 Cor. 12:7-10).

Paul says that a messenger of Satan was sent against him. When he went to God about it, God said, "My grace is sufficient." In other words, God's divine favor was a sufficient force to be used not only against the enemy, but also, according to Paul, against infirmities, reproaches, needs, persecutions and distresses.

There is more than enough of God's favor to meet every need that we have. In times when there seems to be no way out of a situation, and we wonder what we are going to do, we can declare, "God's divine favor is sufficient for me!" When the favor of God shows up, circumstances change and destinies are altered.

We Are Destined for Victory

Perhaps you recall the story of Joseph from the Old Testament. Joseph's destiny was fulfilled by the favor of God. When his older brothers became jealous of Joseph, they sold him into slavery. He was taken to Egypt, where the captain of Pharaoh's guard purchased him. Then the story takes an unexpected turn:

> The LORD was with Joseph, and he was a successful man; and he was in the house of his master the Egyptian. And

> his master saw that the LORD was with him and that the LORD made all he did to prosper in his hand. So Joseph found favor in his sight, and served him. Then he made him overseer of his house, and all that he had he put under his authority. So it was, from the time that he had made him overseer of his house and all that he had, that the LORD blessed the Egyptian's house for Joseph's sake; and the blessing of the LORD was on all that he had in the house and in the field. Thus he left all that he had in Joseph's hand, and he did not know what he had except for the bread which he ate (Gen. 39:2-6).

Now here's a man who is supposed to be a slave, and his master has turned everything over to him. Joseph's master doesn't even know what all he possesses, but he knows that Joseph does. That's pretty extraordinary trust! Because the favor of God was upon Joseph, the house of the Egyptian was blessed, and Joseph flourished in a difficult situation. Joseph's destiny was altered because of the favor of God.

But then the plot twists again. The Bible says that Joseph was a handsome man—so handsome that his master's wife took notice of him. Although she tried continually to seduce him, Joseph's integrity would not allow him to compromise.

> So it was, as she spoke to Joseph day by day, that he did not heed her, to lie with her or to be with her.
>
> But it happened about this time, when Joseph went into the house to do his work, and none of the men of the

> house was inside, that she caught him by his garment, saying, "Lie with me." But he left his garment in her hand, and fled and ran outside. . . .
>
> So she kept his garment with her until his master came home. Then she spoke to him with words like these, saying, "The Hebrew servant whom you brought to us came in to me to mock me; so it happened, as I lifted my voice and cried out, that he left his garment with me and fled outside."
>
> So it was, when his master heard the words which his wife spoke to him, saying, "Your servant did to me after this manner," that his anger was aroused. Then Joseph's master took him and put him into the prison, a place where the king's prisoners were confined (Gen. 39:10-12,16-20).

Notice that there is no indication that Joseph ever defended himself. He never told his master, "Your wife is lying." He didn't have to defend himself, because he knew the favor of God was on him. He knew the favor of God would vindicate him, and that's just what happened.

> But the LORD was with Joseph and showed him mercy, and He gave him favor in the sight of the keeper of the prison. And the keeper of the prison committed to Joseph's hand all the prisoners who were in the prison; whatever they did there, it was his doing. The keeper of the prison did not look into anything that was under Joseph's

> authority, because the LORD was with him; and whatever he did, the LORD made it prosper (Gen. 39:21-23).

Once again, the favor of God was with Joseph to fulfill the course of his destiny. Joseph got thrown into prison, and he became the warden. Now, that's favor. Nothing could stop this man from being victorious, despite how low his circumstances had taken him. The favor of God kept bringing him to the top—and the best was yet to come.

NOTHING COULD STOP JOSEPH FROM BEING VICTORIOUS, DESPITE HOW LOW HIS CIRCUMSTANCES HAD TAKEN HIM. THE FAVOR OF GOD KEPT BRINGING HIM TO THE TOP—AND THE BEST WAS YET TO COME.

Two years after Joseph was imprisoned, Pharaoh had a disturbing dream that no one could interpret for him. Pharaoh's butler told him of a young Hebrew man, Joseph, who could interpret dreams. Joseph was summoned from the prison, and he interpreted the dream, providing Pharaoh with an answer that gave him peace. Once again, the favor of God altered Joseph's destiny.

> So the advice was good in the eyes of Pharaoh and in the eyes of all his servants. And Pharaoh said to his servants, "Can we find such a one as this, a man in whom is the Spirit of God?"

> Then Pharaoh said to Joseph, "Inasmuch as God has shown you all this, there is no one as discerning and wise as you. You shall be over my house, and all my people shall be ruled according to your word; only in regard to the throne will I be greater than you." And Pharaoh said to Joseph, "See, I have set you over all the land of Egypt."
>
> Then Pharaoh took his signet ring off his hand and put it on Joseph's hand; and he clothed him in garments of fine linen and put a gold chain around his neck. And he had him ride in the second chariot which he had; and they cried out before him, "Bow the knee!" So he set him over all the land of Egypt (Gen. 41:37-43).

Joseph spent years of his life as a captive after his brothers turned against him. He was sold into slavery and then thrown into prison. One would never expect him to end up in the presence of Pharaoh himself, much less have the entire land of Egypt placed under his oversight. But Joseph emerged victorious, because the favor of God was on his life—and all of this happened before he was 36 years old.

To be clear, having the favor of God on our lives does not exempt us from trials. It does not mean we will never have another problem or be faced with another challenge. (Remember, Joseph faced the problem of his master's wife's advances and the trial of imprisonment, even after God's favor had clearly been at work in his life.) What it does mean is that we will not be destroyed by trials, problems or challenges. We will not be defeated; rather, we will be victorious.

Joseph is by no means the only example in the Bible of someone who found favor in the sight of God and man. Genesis 6:8 tell us that Noah "found grace in the eyes of the LORD." Ruth found favor with Boaz, saying, "Why have I found favor in your eyes, that you should take notice of me?" (Ruth 2:10). The young boy, Samuel, "grew in stature, and in favor both with the LORD and men" (1 Sam. 2:26).

In each instance, people overcame their trials because of the favor of God on their lives. Noah literally faced a storm of proportions that the world had never seen. Ruth not only lost her husband, but also left her family and all that was familiar to her to live in a foreign land. Samuel's mother had given him over as a young child to be raised and mentored by Eli the priest.

These and many other biblical stories describe people who faced dire circumstances and came through victoriously because of God's favor upon their lives. One of the most memorable of these accounts tells of Job, a man who lost everything he had: his children, his property, and eventually his health. The first 42 chapters of the book of Job describe what may be the greatest personal crisis ever recorded in history, all of which happened in a period of only 9 to 12 months. Despite his terrible suffering, Job made this statement in a prayer to God: "You have granted me life and favor, and Your care has preserved my spirit" (Job 10:12).

At the time Job made this declaration, he was still in the midst of his trial; God did not restore him until some time later. One time, when I was reading these words of Job, the Spirit of God asked me, "Do you suppose the declaration Job made in the midst of that adversity had anything to do with the turnaround in his life?" Even as everything around him was falling apart, Job declared that the favor of God was upon him. In the natural, it would have made sense for him to just give up on God and quit, as his wife suggested that he do. Instead, he declared that he had been granted the favor of God.

Psalm 84:11 says, "The Lord God is a Sun and Shield; the Lord bestows [present] grace and favor and [future] glory (honor, splendor, and heavenly bliss)! No good thing will He withhold from those who walk uprightly" (*AMP*). Psalm 30:5 tells us, "His favor is for a lifetime" (*NASB*). Could it be that in the midst of adversity, the key to our victory lies in declaring God's favor in our lives? If God's favor brought victory to all of these people under the old covenant, how much more so will it bring favor to us who have a new covenant founded on promises of grace?

Declaring God's Grace and Favor

It's not enough simply to have a revelation of the importance of God's favor—that is, just to recognize that the favor of God has the power to transform our lives. We also need a revelation of the importance of declaring that favor. There's a divine connection between our declaring the favor of God and the manifestation of that favor. Not a day goes by in which I'm not declaring the favor of God over my life, whether I'm believing God for an airplane or looking for a parking space.

Most of us face challenges—some large, some small—on a regular basis. Oftentimes, we refer to the larger challenges as mountains. For instance, we may describe ourselves as facing a mountain of debt. When we are in such a situation, that mountain will talk to us. It will keep us up all night, trying to convince us that it's too big to deal with and that it's been with us too long for us ever to get rid of it. Truth be told, in the natural we may not have the ability to change our circumstances. But Jesus said we have to talk to our mountains: "For assuredly, I say to you, whoever says to this mountain, 'Be removed and be cast into the sea,' and does not doubt in his heart, but believes that those things he says will be done, he will have whatever he says" (Mark 11:23).

There's a familiar verse in Zechariah that says, "'Not by might nor by power, but by My Spirit,' says the LORD of hosts" (Zech. 4:6). Most of us stop reading at that point, but verse 7 teaches us something crucial about God's favor and the mountains in our lives: "Who are you, O great mountain? Before Zerubbabel you shall become a plain! And he shall bring forth the capstone with shouts of 'Grace, grace to it!' "

According to the Word of God, we are to shout grace, or God's favor, to our mountains. When we declare and shout divine favor to the obstacles we face, we are speaking words of faith, just as Jesus instructed us to do. We're expressing our faith in the favor of God to move that mountain.

The apostle Paul's revelation of favor became a revelation of the power of declaring that favor over the lives of those to whom he ministered. Paul wrote 13 of the 27 epistles, or letters, contained in the New Testament. In each one, he began with a greeting of grace, or divine favor, and he usually concluded with a reminder to his readers that the grace of the Lord Jesus Christ would be with them all.

In his letter to the Romans, Paul wrote, "Grace [divine favor] to you and peace from God our Father and the Lord Jesus Christ" (Rom. 1:7). He offered the same greeting to the church at Corinth (see 1 Cor. 1:3; 2 Cor. 1:2). Concluding his letter to the Galatians, Paul wrote, "The grace [divine favor] of our Lord Jesus Christ be with your spirit. Amen" (Gal. 6:18).

WHEN WE SHOUT DIVINE FAVOR TO THE OBSTACLES WE FACE, WE ARE SPEAKING WORDS OF FAITH. WE'RE EXPRESSING OUR FAITH IN THE FAVOR OF GOD TO MOVE THAT MOUNTAIN.

Time and time again, we see Paul declaring God's favor over the Church, the Body of Christ. He was endeavoring to cause his fellow believers to receive a revelation of God's favor. He wanted them to understand that the favor of God brings with it blessing, prosperity, and victory over every adversity. He wanted them to understand that they didn't have to be poor anymore, they didn't have to be sick anymore, and they didn't have to live "under the circumstances." Neither do we.

The Early Church faced its share of challenges. Those believers had to deal with unthinkable opposition and persecution, but God blessed them in the midst of their trials. The Word says, "With great power the apostles gave witness to the resurrection of the Lord Jesus. And great grace [divine favor] was upon them all. Nor was there anyone among them who lacked" (Acts 4:33-34).

When the favor of God—or, as the Scripture actually says, His "great favor"—is manifesting in the lives of His people the way He desires it to be, there will be no lack among them. Great favor was upon the Early Church, with remarkable results. We should expect nothing different today.

The Word of God says that we are all partakers of God's grace, or divine favor (see Phil. 1:7). The Word also says that, as God's children, we are His heirs:

> For as many as are led by the Spirit of God, these are sons of God. For you did not receive the spirit of bondage again to fear, but you received the Spirit of adoption by whom we cry out, "Abba, Father." The Spirit Himself bears witness with our spirit that we are children of God, and if children, then heirs—heirs of God and joint heirs with Christ (Rom. 8:14-17).

There was a time when I didn't know that I was an heir of God and a joint heir with Jesus Christ. I was raised in a Christian home, and my family was very faithful to the church we attended; I was even nominated for the title of Mr. Vacation Bible School. Of course, I only went because my mama made me go, but still, I don't remember ever not believing that Jesus was the Son of God. I've always believed that He was crucified and raised from the dead, and that He is coming back. You know, a person can believe all of these things and still never make Jesus Lord of his life. I heard the call of God in 1957, at the age of 11, as I watched Oral Roberts on television. But I didn't completely surrender my life to Jesus until February 1969.

It was through the ministry of Kenneth Copeland that I began to learn about righteousness, faith, and the fact that we are joint heirs with Christ. I'll never forget how revealing and exciting the Bible became for Carolyn and me as we began learning these truths and applying them to our lives. (To be perfectly honest, Carolyn knew a little more than I did at the time, but it was still a wonderful experience for us to learn and grow together.)

I remember one book in particular that made a big impact on me: *The Blood Covenant* by E.W. Kenyon. I can still picture that book today: It had a red cover and was small enough to fit perfectly in my shirt pocket. The day the book arrived in the mail, I started reading it, and I could not put it down. The information in that book was so exciting that I almost started jumping on my living room furniture. I carried that little book around with me for weeks, and every time I had a break or a few extra moments, I sat down and read from it.

The next revelation I received came as the result of reading another book: *Redeemed from the Curse* by Kenneth E. Hagin. For the first time, I learned that I was redeemed from every sickness and every disease, as Hagin directed my attention to this passage of Scripture: "Christ has redeemed us from the curse of the law, having become a curse for us (for it is written, 'Cursed is everyone who hangs on a tree'), that the blessing of Abraham might come upon the Gentiles in Christ Jesus, that we might receive the promise of the Spirit through faith" (Gal. 3:13-14). I began constantly reading these verses in Galatians and then turning to Deuteronomy 28 to read about the blessing of Abraham and to see all of the curses from which I had been redeemed. I spent so much time reading these Scriptures, it got to the point where my Bible automatically fell open to Galatians 3 and Deuteronomy 28.

We've already looked at the blessings that obedience to God and His Word brings (see Deut. 28:2-8). As I continued my reading in Deuteronomy 28, I also learned there was a price to be paid for disobedience:

> But it shall come to pass, if you do not obey the voice of the LORD your God, to observe carefully all His commandments and His statutes which I command you today, that all these curses will come upon you and overtake you:
>
> Cursed shall you be in the city, and cursed shall you be in the country.
>
> Cursed shall be your basket and your kneading bowl.
>
> Cursed shall be the fruit of your body and the produce of your land, the increase of your cattle and the offspring of your flocks.
>
> Cursed shall you be when you come in, and cursed shall you be when you go out (Deut. 28:15-19).

Understanding the nature and extent of the curses from which we have been redeemed makes it even more wonderful to realize that we are heirs of God and joint heirs with Jesus, and that all of the promises made to Abraham are ours to enjoy. I can tell you that for the past 40 years, I have been enjoying being the seed of Abraham and a joint heir with Jesus Christ.

I don't mean to say that I have always enjoyed the fullness of every promise, but I'm working on it, and I'm making progress.

To me, the most exciting promise has been the promise of the favor of God.

WHEN THE FAVOR OF GOD IS ON YOUR LIFE, FAILURE AND DEFEAT ARE NEVER INEVITABLE.

God wants us to experience His favor in every area of our lives. I have discovered that having the favor of God is often the factor that makes the difference between winning and losing—between success and failure. When the favor of God is on your life, failure and defeat are never inevitable. As we have seen, that doesn't mean we won't have challenges. Joseph and Job had challenges, the Early Church had challenges, Abraham had challenges, and we will also have challenges. But if we are determined never to give up and to wait for the favor of God, then the favor of God will make us winners—just as it did for the faithful men and women we read about in the Bible.

3

WE HAVE A HERITAGE OF FAVOR

Before God ever spoke forth the words "let there be light," setting in motion the creation of all things that exist, He had a marvelous plan for mankind.

As Paul wrote in his letter to the Galatians, that plan was for all people to be blessed: "And the Scripture, foreseeing that God would justify the Gentiles by faith, preached the gospel to Abraham beforehand, saying, 'In you all the nations shall be blessed.' So then those who are of faith are blessed with believing Abraham" (Gal. 3:8-9).

The covenant God made with Abraham extended to both his natural and his spiritual posterity. Abraham's natural lineage included his son Isaac and his grandson Jacob—who later became Israel, after whom the whole Hebrew nation is named. The term "Gentile" applies to all non-Jewish people, tribes and nations. By faith in Jesus Christ, Gentiles become the spiritual seed of Abraham, as Paul goes on to explain:

> Christ has redeemed us from the curse of the law, having become a curse for us (for it is written, "Cursed is everyone who hangs on a tree"), that the blessing of Abraham might come upon the Gentiles in Christ Jesus, that we might receive the promise of the Spirit through faith. . . . Now to Abraham and his Seed were the promises made. He does not say, "And to seeds," as of many, but as of one, "And to your Seed," who is Christ. . . . And if you are Christ's, then you are Abraham's seed, and heirs according to the promise (Gal. 3:13-14,16,29).

The Bible tells us that if you and I belong to Christ—if we've made Jesus the Lord of our lives—then we "are Abraham's seed, and heirs according to the promise." In other words, whatever God promised to Abraham, He has also promised to us, as we see in Romans 4:16: "Therefore it is of faith that it might be according to grace [divine favor], so that the promise might be sure to all the seed." The apostle Paul tells us that these promises are sure to the seed—or as we might say today, God's promises are a sure thing.

God intends for us to enjoy the fullness of every blessing that He promised to His people in Deuteronomy 28. As heirs of God's promise, these blessings are our heritage. If we are living without the fulfillment of God's promised blessings in our lives, then either we lack an understanding of our heritage or we are simply ignoring the promise that comes to us through our covenant with God.

Genesis 12 contains a particular promise that God made to Abraham—one that applies to us as Abraham's spiritual seed.

God said, "I will make you a great nation; I will bless you and make your name great; and you shall be a blessing" (Gen. 12:2). The *Amplified* version of this Scripture says, "I will bless you [with abundant increase of favors]." In other words, God promised to increase His favor in Abraham's life.

AN ABUNDANT INCREASE IN FAVOR BROUGHT GOOD THINGS INTO ABRAHAM'S LIFE, AND IT WILL DO THE SAME FOR US.

An abundant increase in favor brought good things into Abraham's life, and it will do the same for us. This kind of abundant favor is our heritage; it is available for us because we are the seed of Abraham. We can't even imagine the good things God's favor will accomplish in our lives, because God "is able to do exceedingly abundantly above all that we ask or think" (Eph. 3:20).

As the Bible unfolds Abraham's story, we see that God's favor on his life caused him to become a very successful, prosperous and powerful man. No enemy could defeat him as he walked in the favor of God. Regardless of where he was or the circumstances he was facing, Abraham came through victoriously every time. At one point God said to him, "Get out of your country, from your family and from your father's house, to a land that I will show you" (Gen. 12:1). When Abraham left his family and his country, he ended up right in the middle of the desert—but God still made him a winner. Of the end of Abraham's life, the Bible says that

"Abraham was now old and well advanced in years, and the LORD had blessed him in every way" (Gen. 24:1, *NIV*).

God's intent in establishing a covenant with Abraham was to create a channel by which He could bring blessing into Abraham's life. Through the promise made to Abraham, God also has a channel through which to bring blessing into our lives. God wants us to walk in divine favor—the kind of favor that opens doors men say cannot be opened.

Please remember that walking in divine favor does not mean we will never have any problems, face any opposition, or experience any hurts. The point I'm making is simply that if we take the time to gain an understanding of our heritage of favor and then determine to walk in that favor on a daily basis, we will experience God moving in our lives in new and powerful ways.

God Is Disposed to Show Favor

The earliest record of God's interaction with mankind paints a beautiful picture of His very nature, which is disposed to show favor:

> Then God blessed them, and God said to them, "Be fruitful and multiply; fill the earth and subdue it; have dominion over the fish of the sea, over the birds of the air, and over every living thing that moves on the earth" (Gen. 1:28).

God's grace and favor were manifested in the first blessing He pronounced over the man and woman whom He had created in His image: be fruitful, multiply, fill the earth, subdue it and have dominion. Within this one blessing, we see the very heart of God and the great favor that He has bestowed upon mankind. However, many people—even many Christians—are still in need of a revelation of this favor.

I remember flying back to Fort Worth after ministering at a large meeting in Tulsa, Oklahoma. When I took the middle seat in my assigned row, a woman in her sixties was already in the seat by the window. We smiled and said hello to each other, and then I sat quietly while the rest of the passengers boarded, including a group of people who had attended the meeting where I had just preached.

When they saw me, they greeted me with, "Hello, Brother Jerry!" and "How are you, Brother Jerry?" and "We sure enjoyed hearing you preach this week."

After I had exchanged a few pleasantries with the group, and they had taken their seats, the woman beside me turned and said, "I assume you must be a minister."

"Yes, madam, I am," I told her.

"Well, I'm glad to know that," she said, "because I need prayer, and I need it right now."

I listened as she told me about something she was going through. When she finished, I talked to her about the favor of God and explained the impact it could have on her life. Then I prayed for her. Afterward, she commented about how wonderful it must be to be loved and respected by so many people. I said, "Well, madam, all I can tell you is that it's the favor of God that I talked to you about; and it is an honor to have His favor." I believe that woman went home with a brand-new revelation of God's favor.

Sometimes when Carolyn and I get to thinking about the favor of God, we're amazed. We're not any different from anybody else, but God has blessed the work of our hands in amazing ways. He has definitely fulfilled His promises in our lives! In return, we have spent the past 40-plus years striving to fulfill a promise we made to God when we first started in ministry. We promised Him that no matter how far this ministry went, no matter how big it got, and no matter how well known we might become, we would remain the same people we were then. We determined never to become high-minded or to forget those who helped us get where we were going. Instead, we would always show the same favor to others that God had shown to us. That promise is the reason I still go to preach in small churches that may have no more than 50 people in them.

Recently, I went to just such a church. The pastors—a married couple—were up in age, and the church was in a bind financially, yet they did everything they could to take care of me while I was there. Before leaving home, I had decided that I would take care of my own expenses—and whatever the offering was, large or small, I would give it back to that precious couple and plant it into their lives as a seed.

It turned out that the offering they received the night I spoke was the biggest they had ever had in that small congregation. The pastor was delighted as he handed me a check just prior to my departure. I looked at him and asked, "Now, Pastor, is this check all mine?"

"Oh, yes, Brother Jerry," he said, "it's all yours."

"You mean it's mine with no strings attached, and I can do with it whatever I want?"

"That's right, Brother Jerry."

I took a pen, endorsed the check, and then handed it back to the pastor and said, "Now this check goes to you and your wife; it's yours."

When he asked me why I was giving them the check, I said, "Just call it favor . . . It's the favor of God."

God created us in His image, and if He is disposed to show us His favor, should we not also be disposed to show favor to others? As we sow seeds of favor into the lives of those around us, we will begin to grow in favor in our own lives, just as Jesus did. The Bible says, "Jesus increased in wisdom and stature, and in favor with God and men" (Luke 2:52). If Jesus had the ability to increase in favor with God and man, then so do we.

Walking in the favor of God brings pleasure to our lives. Psalm 5:12 says, "For You, O LORD, will bless the righteous; with favor You will surround him as with a shield." The *Amplified* version of this Scripture puts it this way: "As with a shield You will surround him with goodwill (pleasure and favor)." Despite what some Christians might tell you, God does not object to our having pleasure in this life. As a matter of fact, being a believer should be fun. After all, Jesus prayed for His disciples "that they may have My joy fulfilled in themselves" (John 17:13).

As Jesus' prayer suggests, our joy is meant to be a reflection of His own joy. The Messianic prophecy of Isaiah says of Jesus that "the pleasure of the LORD shall prosper in His hand" (Isa. 53:10). Living a life characterized by joy and godly pleasure is another way that we show forth the image of God in which we were created.

The Word of God also says, "The wicked plots against the just, and gnashes at him with his teeth. The Lord laughs at him, for He sees that his day is coming" (Ps. 37:12-13). When we are surrounded by God's shield of pleasure and favor, He actually laughs at the wicked plots that come against us. We can do the same thing.

WHEN WE ARE SURROUNDED BY GOD'S SHIELD OF PLEASURE AND FAVOR, HE ACTUALLY LAUGHS AT THE WICKED PLOTS THAT COME AGAINST US.

I have always enjoyed laughing, and I get pleasure from making others laugh; it's just part of my nature. Our home was filled with laughter when I was growing up, but I knew that when I got to church I was to leave the fun and laughter at the door. At our church, humor had no place in religion. I remember thinking, *If I truly give my life to Jesus, I'll never laugh again.* But then, in 1969, I met Kenneth Copeland, a young preacher who made people laugh and then delivered the truth in such a way that it got right down into your spirit. I remember telling Carolyn, "That guy is funny; I can't believe he's a preacher."

I didn't know someone could be both funny and a preacher; I'd never seen anything like that before. My religious upbringing had taught me that everything about church had to be quiet and solemn. I knew that God had placed a call on my life, but I thought I would have to change my whole personality in order to answer that call. I could just see myself with a wrinkled, prune-looking face, never laughing, and sitting in a corner all day reading the Bible. *No, thank You, Lord; that's not for me.*

But I learned that God didn't want me to change my personality; rather, He wanted to change my nature. He wanted to take me from death to life, and then He wanted to use the very personality He had given me to touch the lives of others.

Once I began spending more time with God, I discovered that He has a humorous side. I got to thinking about it, and I figured that if God could talk, there wasn't any reason to think He couldn't laugh. As we saw in Psalm 37, God does indeed laugh at His enemy, because He knows his day is coming. His Word also tells us that we "shall laugh at destruction and famine" (Job 5:22).

We have a God who is disposed to show us favor and to surround us with pleasure; therefore, Christianity should be fun. It should be so much fun that sinners become envious and want to join us. Unfortunately, this is not what religion teaches us.

Religion—the Enemy of Favor

Many people confuse Christianity with religion. Religion is, and has always been, about following rules and regulations. Christianity is about a relationship with God, through His Son, Jesus Christ. I have received Jesus as my Lord and Savior, and I love God with all my heart—but I am not a religious man.

Religion insists on strict adherence to the law and completely overlooks the fact that we've been saved by grace: "For by grace [divine favor] you have been saved through faith, and that not of yourselves; it is the gift of God, not of works, lest anyone should boast" (Eph. 2:8-9). With this individual gift of salvation comes a calling from God, "who has saved us and called us with a holy calling, not according to our works, but according to His own purpose and grace [divine favor] which was given to us in Christ Jesus before time began" (2 Tim. 1:9).

Religion causes people to become high-minded and to think they have achieved spiritual stature because of who they are or what they have done. Nothing could be further from the truth. Without Jesus, we are nothing. It is because of Him that we have a relationship with God. It is because of Him that we walk in our heritage of God's divine favor. Religion has absolutely no power to grant us any kind of favor. It does, however, have the ability to cause the Word of God to become ineffective in our lives.

The Pharisees were the religious leaders of Jesus' day. They regarded accurate observance of ceremonial law as the true essence of religious conduct, which is why they challenged Jesus about the behavior of His disciples.

> Then the Pharisees and scribes asked Him, "Why do Your disciples not walk according to the tradition of the elders, but eat bread with unwashed hands?"
>
> He answered and said to them, "Well did Isaiah prophesy of you hypocrites, as it is written: 'This people honors Me with their lips, but their heart is far from Me. And in vain they worship Me, teaching as doctrines the commandments of men.' For laying aside the commandment of God, you hold the tradition of men—the washing of pitchers and cups, and many other such things you do."
>
> He said to them, "All too well you reject the commandment of God, that you may keep your tradition. . . . making the word of God of no effect through your tradi-

tion which you have handed down. And many such things you do" (Mark 7:5-9,13).

According to Jesus, who is the very Word of God manifested in the flesh, those who choose religion ("the tradition of the elders") over relationship will not experience the fullness of God's Word operating in their lives. Religion always esteems tradition above truth.

One of religion's distortions of truth is that it wants to keep people in a sinful state. Religion constantly reminds us that the Bible says, "all have sinned and fall short of the glory of God" (Rom. 3:23). This is true, but thank God, He didn't leave us in this fallen state. He sent Jesus to redeem us from the curse that was brought upon us by Adam's transgression. The blood of Jesus has cleansed us, and we no longer have our old Adamic, sinful nature. We have the very nature of almighty God. We are part of a royal family, and we have a heritage of divine favor.

Many Christians live way below their privileges as children of God because they don't know that they're highly favored of God. Therefore, they don't expect good things to happen to them.

I remember when Oral Roberts first began telling people to expect that something good was going to happen. Religious people rose up and said, "How dare you say such a thing?" I've actually had people get mad at me because they think I'm too positive; they accuse me of being "a positive thinker." I don't mind being called that, because Jesus is a great example of a positive thinker where the things of God are concerned. What those who have criticized me don't understand is that I'm not just dealing with the power of positive thinking; I'm dealing with the power of revelation regarding the favor of God. Once you have something revealed to you from the Word of God, it will most definitely cause your thinking to become positive.

God has always wanted His relationship with mankind to be one in which He pours out His grace—His divine favor—and blessing. He told Moses to instruct Aaron, the priest, to pronounce the following blessing over all of Israel: "The LORD bless you and keep you; the LORD make His face shine upon you, and be gracious to you; the LORD lift up His countenance upon you, and give you peace" (Num. 6:24-26).

GOD HAS ALWAYS WANTED HIS RELATIONSHIP WITH MANKIND TO BE ONE IN WHICH HE POURS OUT HIS GRACE—HIS DIVINE FAVOR—AND BLESSING.

What was Aaron doing each time he pronounced this blessing? He was declaring God's divine favor over the people, and in so doing, he was demonstrating God's love for them. In today's terms, we might say Aaron was showing the people that they were the object of God's love and affection.

I don't know anyone who doesn't enjoy being loved. I know I am the object of my wife's affection, and she knows she is the object of my affection. It's been that way between us throughout our marriage, and it's not going to change. My children are also the object of my affection, and so are my grandchildren. They all know they are loved.

Sadly, there are many Christians who do not understand they are the object of God's affection. They have become so caught up in the rules and regulations of religious tradition that their Christianity has become nothing more than a mechanical exercise. They go to church on Sunday, and perhaps they are even involved in various religious activities—but they have no joy because they have no relationship with God. They have no intimacy with their Savior.

The solution to this problem is as easy as accepting the Bible's best-known verse: "For God so loved the world that He gave His only begotten Son, that whoever believes in Him should not perish but have everlasting life" (John 3:16).

Once people understand the simple truth that they are loved and highly favored by God, who gave His Son that they might know His great grace and favor, they are instantaneously freed from the bondage of religion to truly enjoy their Christianity.

We Are God's Handiwork

The psalmist wrote, "O LORD, our Lord, how excellent is Your name in all the earth, who have set Your glory above the heavens!" (Ps. 8:1). As he begins to think about and dwell on the handiwork of God, this man becomes overwhelmed by just how marvelous and magnificent God is in His creative ability.

As he continues thinking about God's vast creation, the psalmist goes on to say, "When I consider Your heavens, the work of Your fingers, the moon and the stars, which You have ordained, what is man that You are mindful of him, and the son of man that You visit him? For You have made him a little lower than the angels, and You have crowned him with glory and honor" (Ps. 8:3-5).

While it is wonderful to know that God crowned mankind with glory and honor, most of us don't grasp the full meaning of this Scripture because the text that reads "You have made him a little lower than the angels" is a mistranslation. According to Hebrews 1:14, angels are "ministering spirits sent forth to minister for those who will inherit salvation." As heirs of salvation, we could not have been created lower than those who are sent to minister in our behalf.

What the psalmist actually wrote is this: "You have made him a little lower than *Elohim*, and You have crowned him with glory and honor." *Elohim* is a Hebrew word that means "God." In reality, the Word says that we have been made a little lower than God, our Creator.

A creator is always greater than his creation, but let's remember what God said about His creation: "Let Us make man in Our image, according to Our likeness" (Gen. 1:26). The Genesis account of creation goes on to say that "God created man in His own image; in the image of God He created him; male and female He created them" (Gen. 1:27). After God had formed the body of man, He breathed into his nostrils the breath (inspiration, soul, spirit) of life, and man became a living being (see Gen. 2:7), created in the image of God.

Religious tradition would have us believe that we are worms in God's sight, nothing more than a bunch of old sinners barely getting by on the shoestring of grace. If this were true, it would mean that the blood Jesus shed on the cross didn't work and that it has no power today. But the blood of Jesus did work, and it is as powerful today as it was at Calvary. By God's divine grace and favor, we have been crowned with glory and honor—and God intends for us to walk continuously in that honor.

BY GOD'S DIVINE GRACE AND FAVOR, WE HAVE BEEN CROWNED WITH GLORY AND HONOR—AND GOD INTENDS FOR US TO WALK CONTINUOUSLY IN THAT HONOR.

Throughout the years I've been in ministry, I've encountered many people who have not enjoyed the victories that belong to them, because they have such a poor self-image. Jesus said we should love others as we love ourselves, but I've found that there are a lot of folks who don't even love themselves. The Word directs us to "be strong in the grace that is in Christ Jesus" (2 Tim. 2:1). In other words, we are not to be weak where the favor of God is concerned. We are to be strong and have a positive outlook regarding the favor of God. Many believers, especially those who were not raised in environments where they were praised and encouraged, have difficulty grasping this truth.

Carolyn and I were driving home following dinner one evening when she noticed a bumper sticker on the car in front of us. At first glance it appeared to be one of those positive messages announcing that a child is an honor student at some particular school. But when we looked closer, we read these words: "My child is the number one inmate at the Texas state prison." Now, I'm sure that when those people put that sticker on their car, they did it because they thought it was funny—not because they wanted their child to end up in prison. But the point I want to make is this: When a child grows up hearing words like these being spoken over his or her life, it's quite likely that the child will fulfill what has been decreed.

I've had people ask me, "Do you mean that confessing things like that over my children will cause them to turn out that way?"

My answer is always, "They will unless there's divine intervention." The Word of God teaches us to "train up a child in the way he should go, and when he is old he will not depart from it" (Prov. 22:6). The words we speak over our children, good or bad, carry great power. This is why it is so important to declare God's divine favor over our families on a daily basis.

For those who were not brought up hearing words of grace and divine favor spoken over them, I have good news. The Word of God can be used to tear down "arguments and every high thing that exalts itself against the knowledge of God, bringing every thought into captivity to the obedience of Christ" (2 Cor. 10:5). Paul described the Word of God as "living and powerful, and sharper than any two-edged sword, piercing even to the division of soul and spirit, and of joints and marrow, and is a discerner of the thoughts and intents of the heart" (Heb. 4:12). Through the Word of God, we have the ability to change our thinking and to cause it to line up with what God says about us. God says that we are made in His image. We have been crowned with glory and honor. We walk in authority and dominion.

Armed with the name of Jesus and the Word of God, we can take authority over the untruths and disheartening circumstances that seem to be controlling our lives. God's favor can change even the most impossible-looking situation.

Remember Psalm 84:11? "The LORD God is a sun and shield; the LORD will give grace [divine favor] and glory; no good thing will He withhold from those who walk uprightly." I don't care how dire your circumstances may be or how much money you may need or how negative a report you may have received from the doctor or the lawyer—or even how many times you may have been told you would never amount to anything. When the favor of God comes on the scene, failure and defeat are no longer inevitable. The favor of God brings good things into your life; it brings prosperity.

When we truly understand just how important we are to our heavenly Father, doubt and insecurity will vanish, and we will walk in the fullness of the heritage of favor that is ours in Jesus Christ.

4

GROWING IN GOD'S FAVOR

My wife tells me all the time, "Jerry, you walk in more favor than anybody I've ever met. God is always doing something for you."

My usual response is: "I can't help it if He loves me and I'm his favorite child." I don't mean this in an arrogant way. It's just that I'm confident in the knowledge of who I am in Christ and the fact that I walk in the favor of God.

The apostle Paul gave Timothy, whom he considered to be a son in the faith, these words of encouragement: "You therefore, my son, be strong in the grace that is in Christ Jesus" (2 Tim. 2:1). Paul was instructing Timothy to be strong in the divine favor that was his in Jesus Christ. He wanted him to be strong in this favor and to come to expect its manifestation in his life.

As our Father, God wants us to become highly developed in our expectancy of His favor manifesting in our lives. He wants this for us not only when we are in times of need, but also on an everyday basis. I can assure you that once you begin to experience God's favor on a consistent basis, it won't be long before you'll be declaring that you are His favorite child. Don't worry; in the expanse of God's vast love, there is plenty of room for each of us to be His favorite child.

Carolyn and I were in Singapore one time, and I had the opportunity to try on some Hugo Boss suits. The sales associate selected a beautiful sports coat for me to try on. He took great care to see that it fit properly. It really was a perfect fit, and I wanted to buy it, so I asked how much it cost. When he told me the coat alone cost $1,500, I said, "Get thee behind me, Satan! For $1,500 I don't get any pants?"

"No, sir, just the sports coat."

"You've got to be kidding," I said. "Get this thing off of me."

Please don't misunderstand me. If somebody wants to spend $1,500 for a sports coat, that's fine with me. I'm just not going to pay that much money, because I believe that with the favor of God, I can have that sports coat without paying full price for it.

Several months later, I was visiting my friend Dan in New York City. I had just been blessed with some money, so I asked if there was a place in the city where I could find a Hugo Boss suit and not have to pay the world's price for it. I remember telling him, "I'm not asking for a preacher's discount; I just believe in getting everything I can for my money."

Dan said, "I've lived here most of my life, and I don't know of any place like that." Turning his attention to more pressing matters, he said, "It's almost noon; how about my wife and I take you to lunch?"

"Okay then," I told him, "let's go eat. We'll just let God work things out where the suit is concerned."

The three of us got in Dan's car and drove across town to a parking garage. Dan explained that we would leave the car there and walk several blocks to the restaurant. When we stepped out of the garage, I had absolutely no idea where I was or what street I was on, so I just kept in step with Dan and his wife. As we turned this way and that, making our way through the crowded streets of New York City, we were all talking nonstop—preaching to one another, testifying to what God was doing in our lives, and talking about the Word.

Finally, Dan said, "Wait a minute! We're going the wrong way. We should have turned left at the last street, and we went right." So we turned around to go the other direction.

That's when Dan's wife said, "I don't believe it—look!" Right in front of us was a men's clothing store, and hanging in the front window was a huge sign that read, "Hugo Boss suits—half price."

When the favor of God manifests in my life, the first thing I do is declare, "That's the favor of God." So that's what I did. The next thing I always do is respond to that favor. So that day, I forgot about lunch and went straight inside that store, where I ended up getting not one, but four Hugo Boss suits. I'm telling you, they were fine-looking suits—and I didn't have to pay the world's price for them.

But the best part of that experience was that I developed a relationship with the man who helped me with my selection, and he told me he would sell me suits at that price as long as I wanted to buy them. "You don't even have to come here," he said. "We'll just measure you and then we can send them to you anywhere you are."

As we left the store several hours later, my friends said, "Brother Jerry, we've never seen anything like this. How long are you going to be with us, and can we have some of what you've got?"

"I'm going to be here one more day," I told them. "I've got the favor of God on me, and if you get any closer, it'll get on you, too."

The Bible tells us that if we delight ourselves in the Lord, He will give us the desires of our heart (see Ps. 37:4). In this particular instance, I desired a Hugo Boss suit—without the retail price tag—and God gave me what I desired and more. You see, when our lifestyles are pleasing to Him—when we order our lives according to His Word—then our desires are going to be in line with His will for our lives, and that's when the favor of God shows up.

It's important to understand that although the favor of God is available for us to walk in on a consistent basis, it will not come our way if doubt and unbelief fill our thoughts.

ALTHOUGH THE FAVOR OF GOD IS AVAILABLE FOR US TO WALK IN ON A CONSISTENT BASIS, IT WILL NOT COME OUR WAY IF DOUBT AND UNBELIEF FILL OUR THOUGHTS.

The Word of God tells us to "gird up the loins of your mind, be sober, and hope to the end for the grace [divine favor] that is to be brought unto you at the revelation of Jesus Christ" (1 Pet. 1:13, *KJV*). In other words, we have a part to play when it comes to walking in divine favor.

According to the Word of God, our part is to think soberly. Our part is to exercise our faith and believe for the favor of God. What is going on in our heads will make or break us, because our thoughts determine our words, and our words determine our actions.

The *Amplified* version of 1 Peter 1:13 says that we are to "brace up [our] minds" as we hope, or expect, God's favor to be brought to us. *THE MESSAGE* translation says that we are to "put [our] mind[s] in gear." The various translations of this passage indicate that expectancy is not just a spiritual exercise, but a mental one as well.

Becoming Favor-minded

I fully expect the favor of God to come into every situation that I am, or will be, experiencing. I like to describe this mindset as being "favor-minded." In other words, my mind is unchangeably set on the fact that divine favor is coming to me.

Becoming favor-minded doesn't happen automatically when we receive Jesus as our Lord and Savior. The Word tells us that we are responsible for taking control of our minds and thinking soberly, which means we are to think "soundly." I've heard some people argue that it's not possible to think this way, because there's no way for us to control our thoughts. But that's not what the Bible says. We're told to "[cast] down arguments and every high thing that exalts itself against the knowledge of God, bringing every thought into captivity to the obedience of Christ" (2 Cor. 10:5). If the Word of God says we can do something, then we can do it.

We are also told, in Romans 12:2, to "be transformed by the renewing of [our] mind[s], that [we] may prove what is that good and acceptable and perfect will of God." It is the will of God that we walk in His divine favor. This is why it is so important that we renew our minds to this truth. What is going on in our minds, along with what we speak, plays a part in whether we see the favor of God manifest in our circumstances. If Satan can successfully distract us in our thoughts and speech, causing us to focus on the negative, it is highly improbable that we will experience the favor of God. With the absence of God's favor, there is inevitably the absence of peace.

In one of Paul's familiar greetings, he wrote the following: "Grace [divine favor] and peace be multiplied to you in the knowledge of God and of Jesus our Lord" (2 Pet. 1:2). Notice the connection between divine favor and peace. The *Amplified Bible* reads like this: "May grace (God's favor) and peace (which is perfect well-being, all necessary good, all spiritual prosperity, and freedom from fears and agitating passions and moral conflicts) be multiplied to you in [the full, personal, precise, and correct] knowledge of God and of Jesus our Lord."

Paul tells us that we can have the favor of God and the peace of God multiplied in our lives, which will result in freedom from fear. Once, after reading this verse, I wrote the following note in my Bible: "My life is increasing with the divine favor of God and the freedom from all fear."

Fear of what?

Fear that this might not turn out well.

Fear that I might not get the amount of money I need.

Fear that this situation may not result in my good.

The Word of God says that we can multiply and increase in the favor of God. The more I take control of my mind and build upon my awareness and expectancy of God's favor, the less I will have to deal with the fear of failure.

God's favor in our lives means there will be less and less fear. When we continually expect the favor of God to manifest, it's unlikely that we're going to be fearful about the outcome of our situations. We can actually get to the point that fear of failure does not even cross our minds, because we are boldly expectant of the favor of God manifesting in every situation.

One of the Scripture verses I like to meditate on is Hebrews 4:16: "Let us therefore come boldly to the throne of grace, that we may obtain mercy and find grace to help in time of need." Let's think about this for a moment. If there is a throne of grace, we now understand that it's a throne of divine favor—and we are told to come boldly to that throne. We don't have to slip up on the backside of the throne of God, begging for His mercy and His favor, hoping that we are worthy of it. No! We can come boldly to the throne of divine favor for the purpose of obtaining mercy and divine favor in our time of need. In other words, when I go to the throne of divine favor, I expect that when I leave, I will have received the help I need. I expect to have received the divine favor that will change my circumstances.

I challenge you to take this verse in Hebrews and meditate on it. Renew your mind to its truth. Whatever difficult situation you may be facing—financial, marital, family, health—know that you have access to divine favor. You can go boldly to the throne, expecting God to help you with manifestations of His favor.

Developing Faith in the Favor of God

It is imperative that we develop our faith in the favor of God. Knowing that "faith is the substance of things hoped for, the evidence of things not seen" (Heb. 11:1), we learn to expect God's favor as we go boldly to the throne of grace.

In chapter 2, we discussed the importance of declaring God's favor when we face problems of mountainous proportions. Jesus said, "Have faith in God. For assuredly, I say to you, whoever says to this mountain, 'Be removed and be cast into the sea,' and does not doubt in his heart, but believes that those things he says will be done, he will have whatever he says" (Mark 11:22-23). We are to use our faith in the favor of God to speak to those mountains until they become molehills. This is how we exercise and develop our faith in the favor of God.

WE ARE TO USE OUR FAITH IN THE FAVOR OF GOD TO SPEAK TO THOSE MOUNTAINS IN OUR LIVES UNTIL THEY BECOME MOLEHILLS.

I believe the reason some of the mountains we face seem to be so stubborn is that we have not been developing our faith in the favor of God by speaking to them. We can hope they will move, and we can spend countless sleepless nights wondering when they are going to leave. But until we exercise our faith in the favor of God by commanding those mountains to depart, nothing is going to happen.

The more we speak to the mountains in our lives, the more we will see the favor of God manifesting and moving those mountains. In turn, the more we see our mountains move, the greater our faith will become. There is no mountain that can stand against the favor of God, no matter how great it might seem.

As we see the favor of God at work to remove our mountains, it's important to begin thanking God on a daily basis for His favor in our lives. David said, "But You, O Lord, are a God full of compassion, and gracious, longsuffering and abundant in mercy and truth" (Ps. 86:15). The word "gracious" in this verse means that God is "favorable, or disposed to show favor." There's one thing I want to point out about David: He continually praised God for His goodness, His mercy, His grace, and the favor that was on his life.

I challenge you to watch for and expect God's favor, and to believe for it to manifest every day of your life. When it does, no matter how small that manifestation may seem in your estimation, give God praise for it. Immediately declare, "That's the favor of God!"

There are those who will say, "You just never know what God is going to do." These people believe that whatever will be, will be. They stumble through life, taking hard knocks and hoping that everything will eventually be okay. But as Christians, we have the right to believe for divine favor.

When the Bible talks about the elect of God, it's talking about us. Jesus said, "You did not choose Me, but I chose you"

(John 15:16). We have been chosen, and we have been crowned with glory and honor. We ought to be walking in that glory and honor, knowing who we are in Christ, and never just taking whatever the devil thinks he can dish out.

I believe that developing faith in the favor of God is something that has been overlooked by many in the Body of Christ. Don't misunderstand; I'm not talking about going on some ego trip. I'm not talking about getting into some form of arrogance or pride, or being high-minded. I'm talking about developing faith in the fact that the favor of God will turn every adversity in your life into a victory.

I don't know anyone who hasn't at some time been under tremendous pressure and had to deal with a situation that seemed impossible. I know I've experienced this kind of pressure many times. But each time I stood in faith and declared the favor of God, I've watched what was once an overwhelming situation turn into a testimony of victory.

You know, the devil would like it if we forgot those testimonies. He wants us to stay overwhelmed and in a position where we don't consider the miracles that God has already wrought for us. But the Word of God tells us that "our brethren . . . overcame him [the devil] by the blood of the Lamb and by the word of their testimony" (Rev. 12:10-11). God wants us to remember our victories, and He wants us to rehearse our testimonies.

The Old Testament includes many examples of God performing miracles and bringing victory in the lives of His people. Every time the Israelites experienced a miraculous victory, the first thing God instructed them to do was to place stones at the site of the victory as a memorial—a reminder of what He had done. Every time they came that way again and walked past that place, He wanted them to be reminded of the victory.

Similarly, God wants to use the testimonies of His work in our lives as memorials that help us remember. He wants us to think about our victories, rehearse them, and never forget them. Reminding ourselves about God's miracles in our lives strengthens our faith in the favor of God. Talking about our victories serves as a great weapon against the adversary, particularly when he's endeavoring to overwhelm us with a problem. When we recall the miracles of God and how His divine favor moved formidable mountains, our faith will be energized. Anytime our faith is energized, not only will it move mountains, but it will also overcome the devil.

How to Increase in Favor

In order to get to the place where our faith will move mountains and we have the ability to overcome everything that the world—or the enemy—throws at us, we must increase in favor.

Let's look at 2 Peter 3:18, which instructs us to "grow in the grace and knowledge of our Lord and Savior Jesus Christ." When we translate the word "grace" as "divine favor," what this verse is saying is that we are to grow in divine favor and knowledge of our Lord and Savior Jesus Christ. In other words, the more we grow in the knowledge of Jesus Christ, the more we will increase in the manifestation of the favor of God.

The Word of God tells us that Jesus Himself grew in favor: "And Jesus grew in wisdom and stature, and in favor with God and men" (Luke 2:52, *NIV*). Other translations render "grew" as "increased." If the favor of God increased in Jesus' life, then it can also increase in our lives.

Some people have said to me, "Now, wait a minute, Brother Jerry; that was Jesus." In essence, what they are saying is that Jesus is the only one who can grow in favor. Well, if that is true, then by extension no one but Jesus can increase in wisdom or stature, either. But we all know that it is possible for us to increase in both wisdom and stature. Therefore, it is also possible for us to increase in the favor of God.

Just as we have a part to play in walking in the favor of God, we also have a part to play in increasing in that favor. I have studied what the Word of God has to say about favor for many years, and I have discovered three important keys to our increasing in favor.

Key #1: We Must Consider Our Ways

The psalmist wrote, "I entreated Your favor with my whole heart; be merciful to me according to Your word. I thought about my ways, and turned my feet to Your testimonies" (Ps. 119:58-59). Here is someone who is asking for favor, and he is asking for it with his whole heart. But making the request is only the beginning. Notice that in the very next sentence, the psalmist states what he must do in order to increase in favor. He says, "I thought about my ways."

If we are going to ask for God's favor to be increased, then we need to take an inventory of our ways. Here's another way to say it: To increase in the favor of God, we must make sure that our ways are pleasing to Him. That is what the psalmist did. He asked for favor, and at the same time made a decision to line up his ways with the testimonies of God.

Obviously, our lifestyles have a direct result on how much favor we walk in. The fact that we are born again and in covenant with God opens the door for God's favor. But if our lifestyles are not pleasing to God, then we are not going to increase in favor.

God spoke through the prophet, Haggai, saying, " 'You have sown much, and bring in little; you eat, but do not have enough; you drink, but you are not filled with drink; you clothe yourselves, but no one is warm; and he who earns wages, earns wages to put into a bag with holes.' Thus says the LORD of hosts: 'Consider your ways!' " (Hag. 1:6-7). If we are not experiencing the favor of God in our lives to the extent that it has been promised, we should examine our ways and see if they are pleasing to the Lord.

IF WE ARE NOT EXPERIENCING THE FAVOR OF GOD IN OUR LIVES TO THE EXTENT THAT IT HAS BEEN PROMISED, WE SHOULD EXAMINE OUR WAYS AND SEE IF THEY ARE PLEASING TO THE LORD.

We know that God approved Jesus, who said at the time of Jesus' baptism, "You are my beloved Son, in whom I am well pleased" (Mark 1:11). Another time, as several of the disciples witnessed the transfigured Jesus talking with Moses and Elijah, God spoke again, saying, "This is My beloved Son, in whom I am well pleased" (Matt. 17:5). The favor of God was upon Jesus, not because He was the Son of God, but because His ways were pleasing to God.

We have already established the connection between divine favor and the peace we experience in life. But peace is also the result of our ways being pleasing to the Lord: "When a man's ways please the LORD, He makes even his enemies to be at peace with him" (Prov. 16:7). When I consider my ways and make my lifestyle pleasing to the Lord, I avoid having to fight some battles simply because God makes my enemies to be at peace with me.

If we want to increase in the favor of God, our ways must be pleasing to Him. If there is something in your life that you know by the testimony of the Word and the conviction of the Holy Spirit is not pleasing to God, then take authority over it and remove it from your life. When you do, you will begin to see the favor of God increase in all areas of your life.

KEY #2:
WE MUST HEAR INSTRUCTION

The book of Proverbs has much to say about instruction, and I always like to begin my study with these verses: "Now therefore, listen to me, my children, for blessed are those who keep my ways. Hear instruction and be wise, and do not disdain it. Blessed is the man who listens to me, watching daily at my gates, waiting at the posts of my doors. For whoever finds me finds life, and obtains favor from the LORD" (Prov. 8:32-35).

In this passage, "me" refers to "instruction." Instruction is the speaker; those who seek and wait for instruction will be blessed and obtain favor. Not so for those who despise instruction: "But to the wicked God says: 'What right have you to declare My statutes, or take My covenant in your mouth, seeing you hate instruction and cast My words behind you?'" (Ps. 50:16-17). When we despise instruction, we are in essence abdicating our right to walk in God's statutes and in His covenant.

In order to increase in the favor of God, we must be diligent in searching His Word for instruction. Proverbs 11:27 says that "he who earnestly seeks good finds favor, but trouble will come to him who seeks evil." I especially like the way the *King James* translation reads: "He that diligently seeketh good procureth favour: but he that seeketh mischief, it shall come unto him." So mischief will come to those who seek it, but those who do good shall procure—or get possession of—favor.

There are many people who have accepted Jesus and are therefore going to heaven, but they are not enjoying the favor of God in this life. They live with a barely-get-by mentality and lifestyle, always looking for shortcuts. Rather than seeking instruction in order to achieve excellence in all they do, they seek to do the least amount necessary to get by. I do not enjoy working with people who have what I call an "it's good enough" mentality—who are constantly watching the clock and counting the minutes until it's time to leave. We don't hire people like that in this ministry. Instead, we look for those who make the effort to hear instruction and strive for excellence.

Looking again to the book of Proverbs, we see that "a good man obtains favor from the LORD" (Prov. 12:2) and "he who keeps instruction is in the way of life" (Prov. 10:17). When we encounter people who are constantly disobedient to God's instruction, it's easy to see that they are not walking in much favor. But those who hear God's instructions and determine to be obedient to them will experience His favor. The more we increase in obedience to instruction, the more we will increase in the favor of God.

Key #3:
We Must Get Understanding

In order to increase in God's favor, we must not only consider our ways and be obedient to the instruction we receive, but we must also strive to get understanding. Scripture tells us, "He who despises the word will be destroyed, but he who fears the commandment will be rewarded. The law of the wise is a fountain of life, to turn one away from the snares of death. Good understanding gains favor" (Prov. 13:13-15).

Next to this verse in my study Bible, I wrote, "Never lose your zeal for the Word, never lose your hunger for revelation knowledge, and always desire understanding." While I desire to grow in understanding of the entire Word of God, I know that getting understanding of the favor of God will cause that favor to increase in my life—and it will do the same for you. That is why I have written this book; I want you to have an understanding of God's favor and to experience it on a consistent basis in every area of your life.

Sadly, I hear some Christians say things like, "I'm so tired of studying the Word" or "Why do I have to be in the Word all of the time?" The Word has become irksome to them. They have lost their zeal for it. At one time, these people were strong in the Word, attending every Bible study, buying the latest books and inspirational messages, going to seminars, and being in church on a regular basis. But then their attendance at church and meetings became less frequent, and as a result, they spent less and less time in the Word. They lost their desire for it. When someone loses their desire for the Word, they literally cut themselves off from God's favor.

God wants us to walk in a continuous flow of His favor; but without a Bible-based understanding of favor, we are vulnerable to suffer from the same difficulties the world experiences. I tell people that while the economy may be bad, it doesn't have to stop the favor of God from bringing blessing to our lives.

Oftentimes after I preach this, someone will say, "That may be true for you, but you just don't understand my problem."

My response is always, "Your problem is not the issue. The issue is that you don't understand the power of the favor of God."

I have preached the message of the favor of God all over the world for more than 40 years. I've preached it in places where people live in mud huts with no electricity and no running water. I've watched these people get revelations of the favor of God and eventually get houses, cars and businesses. Before long, they are supporting the work of God in their communities. If understanding the favor of God works in the bush of Africa, it will work right now, right where you are, regardless of your circumstances.

Do you know who has given me the hardest time about preaching this message in countries afflicted with abject poverty? It hasn't been the nationals, or the people who lived there. It has been the religious American missionaries, who say, "You can't preach prosperity in this country, Brother Jerry."

I just smile and ask them, "Why not?"

Invariably, they answer, "Because the people are poor."

That's about as rational as saying that you can't preach salvation someplace because the people are lost. It doesn't make any sense.

You can experience a continuous flow of the favor of God no matter how negative your circumstances might be. Throughout the Bible, we see examples of God's people experiencing various kinds of challenges and tests; even in the most desperate of those situations, when the favor of God manifested, it changed their circumstances into something positive.

I still face challenges just like everyone else does. I'm dealing with some impossible-looking situations at this very moment—and in the natural, there's not a thing I can do to change the circumstances. But being favor-minded changes the way I look at these circumstances, because I know that the favor of God is coming, and I know that I am growing in God's favor.

Growing in the favor of God does not depend on the economy or the doctor's report or where you were born or where you live or your education or any natural fact of life. Growing in the favor of God depends on your first becoming favor-minded, then developing faith in the favor of God, and finally becoming determined to increase in that favor.

5

MOVING TO A HIGHER LEVEL OF FAVOR

The first time Carolyn and I visited the former Soviet Union country of Ukraine, the Berlin wall had just come down. Although Communism was dying out in the region, we could still see the toll it had taken on the land and the people.

The cost of bread changed every day. We'd go to the market and pay a certain price for food one day, and the next day the exact same thing would cost 10 times more—thanks to the Russian mafia. People were given tiny plots of land, which the government allowed them to have to raise their own produce, but the land didn't produce much.

The equipment at the main hospital in the capital city of Kiev looked like stuff American hospitals had discarded in the 1930s. One of the surgeons we met there was making less money than a high school janitor would make in America. The hospital administrator allowed me to put on a gown and surgical mask so that I could observe the surgeons at work; what they were able to accomplish with what little they had was nothing short of miraculous.

When Carolyn and I had completed our mission in Kiev, we flew to Vienna, Austria. Although we had traveled only a few hundred miles, the lifestyle there was markedly different from that in Kiev. Known as the City of Music because of its musical heritage, Vienna had been ranked number one not only for its quality of life, but also for its culture of innovation. Carolyn and I were absolutely stunned at the difference between the two cities.

It saddened us to think that the people over in Ukraine had no idea that this other lifestyle existed such a short distance away. The reason they didn't know was that they were bound by their culture. They had been lied to and told that God didn't exist; therefore, they had never seen or experienced the favor that was available to them through faith in Jesus Christ. They were bound by the beliefs that had been dictated to them by people in authority.

UNFORTUNATELY, MANY BELIEVERS TODAY ARE BOUND BY THEIR CULTURE AND THE BELIEFS THAT HAVE BEEN PASSED DOWN TO THEM.

Unfortunately, many believers today are bound by their culture and the beliefs that have been passed down to them. The Word of God tells us that "as [a man] thinks in his heart, so is he" (Prov. 23:7). The reason so many of God's people do not walk at a higher level of favor in their lives is that they can't get past old mindsets. They can't get past their upbringing, their culture, and the standards of living that were set by their families—particularly if those standards did not line up with the Word of God.

So how do we move beyond these restrictive cultural mindsets to a higher level of favor? As always, the answer is found in the Bible, which instructs us, "Do not be conformed to this world, but be transformed by the renewing of your mind, that you may prove what is that good and acceptable and perfect will of God" (Rom. 12:2).

The *Phillips New Testament* puts it this way: "Don't let the world around you squeeze you into its own mould." The *Good News Translation* tells us, "Do not conform yourselves to the standards of this world." The word "standard" can be defined as "that which is widely recognized as the model of authority." But that's the world's definition. Whatever the world's standard is, we're expected to adapt to it because it's the accepted way of doing things.

Take borrowing money, for example. The Bible says we are to "owe no man any thing" (Rom. 13:8, *KJV*). Carolyn's parents took this verse to heart; they never owed anybody. But that wasn't the way I was brought up. My dad owed everybody. He lived on borrowed money, and by the time I was 18 years old, I'd learned to live on borrowed money, too.

The first loan I ever got was so that I could pay my college tuition. My dad's best friend was the vice president of our local bank, so I went to see him. What I didn't realize was that the man who had gotten my dad into debt was about to get me into debt. When I arrived at his office, he shook my hand, told me to have a seat, and then asked, "So, Jerry, what do you have for collateral?"

I said, "What do you mean?"

"Well, what do you own?"

I told him that the only thing I owned was my 1957 Chevrolet, and then I reminded him that I still lived with my parents. I should have known when he said, "We'll take it!" that the paper he presented to me was not something I should sign my name to. But debt was a way of life in my family, and it became a way of life for me, as well. When Carolyn and I married in 1966, debt was very much a part of my life; that was how I ran my automotive business. Debt was the standard of the world in which I had been raised.

So there I was, a young man with a new wife and a fledgling business, headed down the same path that everybody else in my family was on—and I can tell you that the favor of God was nowhere to be seen on that path.

I had no idea there was any other way to live until 1969, when I got hold of God's Word and discovered that He wanted me to live an abundant life. I learned that there was a better way to live than being in debt all the time. I listened to faith-building messages over and over again, and I began to renew my mind to the Word of God.

I'm not saying that it's a sin to borrow, or that if you're in debt then God doesn't love you. But I am telling you that there is a better way—a higher way—to live. There is another standard.

Let's look again at Romans 12:2. Paul says, "Do not be conformed to this world, but be transformed by the renewing of your mind." Notice that the transformation doesn't begin on the outside. We begin experiencing transformation on the inside, with the renewing of our minds.

In my case, I saw myself getting out of debt before I ever started reducing that debt. I saw myself experiencing better health before I had any outward evidence of it. I most certainly saw myself walking in a higher level of favor before it ever manifested.

The only way you and I can break loose from what others consider to be the standard way to live and move to a higher level of favor is by the renewing of our minds. I began this process several decades ago, and I can tell you that I am not the same man today. The way I live now bears no resemblance to the way I lived before I committed myself to renewing my mind.

THE MESSAGE translation of Romans 12:2 says, "Don't become so well-adjusted to your culture that you fit into it without even thinking." The word "culture" in this verse can be defined as "the attitudes, the opinions, the beliefs, and the behavior patterns that are characteristic of the country or the society in which we live."

The reason so many in the Body of Christ are not experiencing God's best is that they've become so well-adjusted to their culture that they can't even think about a better way of living. If we desire to walk in a higher level of the favor of God, we must be willing to walk away from our culture. Most importantly, we must leave old mindsets behind.

This is exactly what God commanded Abraham to do.

Abraham Is Our Example

Reading the story of Abram, who was later called Abraham, in light of Paul's teaching in Romans 12:2 provides a whole new insight into the Scripture:

> Now the LORD had said to Abram: "Get out of your country, from your family and from your father's house, to a land that I will show you. I will make you a great nation; I will bless you and make your name great; and you shall be a blessing. I will bless those who bless you, and I will curse him who curses you; and in you all the families of the earth shall be blessed." So Abram departed as the LORD had spoken to him, and Lot went with him. And Abram was seventy-five years old when he departed from Haran (Gen. 12:1-4).

God's first instruction to Abraham was to get out of his country, away from his family and his father's house. A country is a particular geographical region with boundaries; its people and its culture also distinguish it. Abraham's father, Terah, was a sun worshiper, a man who didn't know God—and who had raised Abraham in a culture that didn't know or honor God. Terah had passed certain opinions and beliefs down to his son. But God had a different lifestyle planned for Abraham—a lifestyle of faith and favor.

God knew that if Abraham was ever going to enter into the kind of life He had planned for him, he would have to make a departure from his culture. He would have to be willing to move away from his kindred. It's not that God didn't want Abraham to be around his family; He just didn't want their beliefs to hinder Abraham and prevent him from entering into the new mindset that would bring him to the life God had prepared for him.

For many years, I've enjoyed reading one particular commentary, written by theologian Arthur Pink, on the book of Genesis.

Pink points out that God actually spoke to Abraham when he was 70 years old, but Abraham waited until his father died 5 years later to depart—and that the meaning of the word *terah*, which was the name of Abraham's father, is "delay."

The fact that it took Abraham five years to depart after hearing God's call indicates that he had a strong attachment to his father, his family and his culture. Notice that Genesis 12:1 says that the LORD "had said" His words to Abraham. The use of the past perfect tense indicates that God's instructions were given some time prior to Abraham's departure.

The problem with many Christians today is that they've never left their country. I'm not talking about physically removing themselves from the United States; I'm talking about leaving the culturally prevalent ideas, ideals, opinions and beliefs responsible for creating negative mindsets that are contrary to the Word of God.

I had to do what God told Abraham to do. I had to leave my father and his opinions. I'm not saying that my dad was a bad man; he was actually a wonderful, God-loving man. But there were important truths that he didn't know. He'd never been taught the Word of God like many of us have been taught today. Consequently, he was still controlled by the world's standards.

I was born in Vicksburg, Mississippi, on the farm that my grandpa bought in 1927, and where my daddy was raised during the Great Depression. Grandpa owned the farm, and he and Grandma raised cattle and hogs in addition to having their own source of fresh produce. Even though Grandpa saw to it that the family made it through the Depression, the Depression never left my grandpa's thinking. He remained Depression-minded for the rest of his life.

For instance, he buried his money in different places all over the farm. He hardly ever bought anything, and when he did, he paid cash for it. Grandpa was still driving his 1939 Chevrolet in 1957, when my daddy made him buy a '53 Chevy.

There was no indoor plumbing on the farm. To get a drink of water, we had to lower a rope with a bucket tied to the end down into the outdoor well and then crank it back up and take the water inside. When Grandpa finally had a pump installed, I remember thinking that we were now a really uptown and civilized family.

I don't believe my daddy would have ever left Vicksburg if left to his own devices. But God had a plan for my life, and He worked it out so that my parents left the farm and settled in Louisiana. I can't imagine what I'd be like today had I stayed in my grandparents' environment all these years. Because my daddy left his country and his kindred, he moved up to a new level of living—and yet it still wasn't the level of living that God had planned for my life.

Once I learned that God had a different standard for living, I had to make the choice to leave behind the old restrictive mindsets that had been part of my family for generations. I'm telling you, leaving old mindsets behind is not an easy thing to do, particularly when you love your daddy like I did mine, and everything he does represents what you like to do.

So when I began to renew my mind to the Word of God, for the first time in my life a wedge appeared in my relationships with my daddy and my mother. We disagreed about mindsets, opinions and culture. I didn't think I was any better than my parents; I just didn't want to live like them anymore.

It's funny now, but wanting to leave behind old mindsets and my culture got me labeled as a "nut" by some members of my family. Of course, once good things started happening, and everyone saw the favor of God operating in my life, guess who they called when they were in trouble? The nut. They'd say, "He's a nut, but God answers the nut's prayers, so see if you can get him on the phone."

Today, a bunch of my family members are just like me—despite their initial resistance to my strange new ideas.

One time, I happened to be preaching near where one of my cousins lived. I had been particularly close to this cousin while I was growing up, but it had been years since I'd seen him, so I went to visit him while I was in the area.

"They tell me you're a preacher now," he said.

"That's right."

"That's too bad," he told me. "You used to be cool."

I said, "I'm cooler now. I call not going to hell cooler. It's hot down there."

Well, that irritated him, so he said, "Yeah, well, you used to be cool and fun to be with, but I don't think I can hang out with you now. You're a preacher, and we don't have anything in common."

"I'm glad you brought that up," I said. "I've been praying for you, and one of these days you're going to be just like me."

"I don't want to be like you."

"Too late," I said. "I'm already praying. In fact, that's why I'm here. I've come to share the Word with you. When the time comes for you to make Jesus the Lord of your life, do you know how to do it?"

"No, and I don't want to know. It's not going to happen," he insisted.

"I'll tell you what," I said. "You just listen, and then I'll leave you alone. If you will confess with your mouth the Lord Jesus Christ and believe in your heart that God raised Him from the dead, you shall be saved. Good to see you again; looking forward to hearing your testimony."

I left the house, got into my car, and closed the door. The next thing I knew, my cousin banged on the window and repeated, "I don't want to be like you!"

I just smiled and said again, "It's too late." Then I started up the engine and backed down the driveway. All the while, he was following me and hollering, "I don't want to be like you!"

That was the last I saw or heard from my cousin until years later, when I preached at Victory Christian Center in Tulsa, Oklahoma. As I looked out into the audience, I spotted this same cousin, his wife at his side, sitting there and smiling. I knew that look, and after the service I gave him a big hug and said, "You're just like me, aren't you?" He smiled and confirmed that he was indeed just like me.

Since then, he has worked with me for more than 30 years in ministry, serving as my international director. He flies all over the world representing this ministry, overseeing our offices in Europe, Canada, Africa and Australia. And guess what? Some members of the family have called him a nut, too.

As I mentioned before, there was a time when I wasn't as close to my parents as I once had been. I had become a preacher, which pleased them, but they'd never had the opportunity to hear me preach. That is, until one night when I was holding a meeting near their city. I called my mom and dad and asked if they'd like to attend the meeting with me, and they said yes. So I drove over and picked them up.

The power of God showed up at that meeting. Miracles started happening, and lots of people got healed. My dad and mom didn't know Jerry Savelle the preacher—the man who had once been their little boy. They had never seen me like that.

After the service, as we were driving back to their house, my dad couldn't keep his eyes off me. He was riding in the front seat with me, and from time to time he would reach his hand over and just pat me on the leg, saying, "I don't know this boy. Son, God's done something in you. Whatever you've got, son, I want it, too."

Shortly thereafter, my parents became a part of this ministry, where they worked for 20 years until they retired. Anytime God took me to another level, or another dream came to pass, or another vision was fulfilled, my dad expressed how proud he was by standing there, shaking his head and saying, "You are blessed, son. You are blessed."

But you know what? My dad was blessed, too, and so was my mom. In our own ways, each of us had left our country—our culture—where our mindsets were concerned. We were transformed by the renewing of our minds, and as a result we've experienced the blessing of walking in the favor of God every day of our lives.

I promise you that what God has done for me and my family, He can do for you and yours, too.

Pay the Price—Reap the Reward

Obviously, changing your culture and your mindset in order to live by a different standard is going to take some work. It's going to take discipline, and it's going to take "stickability," for lack of a better term. In other words, you've got to stick with it, but I assure you that renewing your mind is well worth the time and effort involved.

Anything worth attaining requires that we pay a price of some kind. We generally don't like that part of the equation. For instance, I'd like to look like Hercules, but do I really want to pay the price it would take to make that happen?

ANYTHING WORTH ATTAINING REQUIRES THAT WE PAY A PRICE OF SOME KIND.

My friend Dennis Tinerino was a four-time Mr. Universe, and he loved the Lord. He also loved to preach, and he became known as "the Sermonator" before he died in 2010. At one point, I owned several horses, and one day when Dennis came by my house, I asked him if he'd like to go horseback riding. He said yes, so I loaded up the horses, and we drove to Benbrook Lake, where there was a beautiful park that was ideal for riding and enjoying other outdoor activities. I had just saddled my horse, and as I started to saddle Dennis's horse, he told me he wanted to ride bareback. Who am I to argue with Mr. Universe?

Dennis hopped onto his horse, and then I watched as he proceeded to take off his shirt. All at once, people all over the park stopped everything they were doing and stared at him. He looked like the movie version of Hercules on a horse.

Although Dennis had lived in California for many years, he'd never lost his New York accent. So he said to me, "Yo, Jerry! Take off your shirt; let's get a tan."

I said, "You've got to be kidding. I am not taking off my shirt and riding next to you. You look like Hercules, and I look like Pee-wee Herman."

Is it fair for somebody to look the way Dennis looked? It is if they are willing to pay the price.

Am I willing to pay the price? No.

I've had the pleasure of meeting Evander Holyfield, who is one of my favorite present-day boxers. Evander looks like he is chiseled out of stone; even his ripples have ripples. One time, not long after Mike Tyson bit his ear off, Evander and I attended a meeting together. While we were on the way to the meeting, I asked him, "Evander, what did you think when Mike bit your ear off?"

He said, "I wanted to bite his ear back, but I knew he was going to get disqualified, and I didn't want to get disqualified too, so I just took control of myself and went to my corner. Once they disqualified him, I thought, *That's the quickest multi-millions I've ever made in my life.*"

Because Dennis Tinerino and Evander Holyfield were willing to pay a price to achieve something most people only dream about, they each reaped the rewards produced by their discipline and stickability.

This is where most of the Body of Christ misses the point. We want a comfortable Christianity. We don't want to have to sacrifice anything. We don't want to have to put out any more effort than is absolutely necessary. Instead, we prefer to just make it by the skin of our teeth. We will never experience the fullness of the favor of God if our attitude says, *What's the least I can do?* We simply cannot have God's best with that kind of a mindset.

WE WILL NEVER EXPERIENCE THE FULLNESS OF THE FAVOR OF GOD IF OUR ATTITUDE SAYS, *WHAT'S THE LEAST I CAN DO*? WE SIMPLY CANNOT HAVE GOD'S BEST WITH THAT KIND OF A MINDSET.

Several years ago, I wrote a book titled *Thoughts: The Battle Between Your Ears*. In this book, I talk about the battlefield of the mind. That's where many of our most important battles take place. We lose these battles if all we do is sit in our living rooms, not engaging.

For instance, how many times have you watched a television program where you see people exercising, eating right and losing weight? You may think, *Wow, that's just what I need to do. I can do that.* But then, by the time the program is over, something else comes to your mind: *I've never been disciplined. I've never been able to lose weight. I can't do that.* The next thing you know, you're going to the kitchen for a piece of pie. You lost the battle of the mind before you even got out of the chair.

That's why it's so important that we renew our minds to what the Word of God has to say. We need to take on the attitude Mary had when she said to the servants at the wedding in Cana, "Whatever He says to you, do it" (John 2:5). Our motto needs to be: "Whatever He says to me, I'm going to do it. I'm going to live a lifestyle of obedience." Anytime we are willing to pay the price of obedience, we will reap the reward of that obedience.

Obedience was the key factor in the deliverance of the children of Israel from their captivity in Egypt. After 430 years of slavery, these people had most certainly been thoroughly assimilated into the culture of their captors. Their mindset was one of subservience. Along with the Egyptians, the Israelites had already experienced the plagues that God had brought against the land in which they were held captive. But then, before God brought about the tenth and final plague, He gave the following instructions to Moses:

> Speak to all the congregation of Israel, saying: "On the tenth of this month every man shall take for himself a lamb, according to the house of his father, a lamb for a household. . . .
>
> "Now you shall keep it until the fourteenth day of the same month. Then the whole assembly of the congregation of Israel shall kill it at twilight. And they shall take some of the blood and put it on the two doorposts and on the lintel of the houses where they eat it. . . .
>
> "For I will pass through the land of Egypt on that night, and will strike all the firstborn in the land of Egypt, both man and beast; and against all the gods of Egypt I will execute judgment: I am the Lord. Now the blood

> shall be a sign for you on the houses where you are. And when I see the blood, I will pass over you; and the plague shall not be on you to destroy you when I strike the land of Egypt" (Exod. 12:3,6-7,12-13).

God was about to bring Israel out of captivity, but in order for Him to accomplish this great task, the people had to be obedient. The price of their freedom was their obedience. To experience deliverance from slavery, they would be required to leave the only culture they had known and venture forth to a place that they did not yet know. They would be required to renew their minds to new customs and a new culture that God Himself would establish in their lives.

> And it came to pass at midnight that the LORD struck all the firstborn in the land of Egypt, from the firstborn of Pharaoh who sat on his throne to the firstborn of the captive who was in the dungeon, and all the firstborn of livestock. So Pharaoh rose in the night, he, all his servants, and all the Egyptians; and there was a great cry in Egypt, for there was not a house where there was not one dead.
>
> Then he called for Moses and Aaron by night, and said, "Rise, go out from among my people, both you and the children of Israel. And go, serve the LORD as you have said. Also take your flocks and your herds, as you have said, and be gone; and bless me also."
>
> And the Egyptians urged the people, that they might send them out of the land in haste. For they said, "We shall

> all be dead." So the people took their dough before it was leavened, having their kneading bowls bound up in their clothes on their shoulders. Now the children of Israel had done according to the word of Moses, and they had asked from the Egyptians articles of silver, articles of gold, and clothing. And the LORD had given the people favor in the sight of the Egyptians, so that they granted them what they requested. Thus they plundered the Egyptians.
>
> Then the children of Israel journeyed from Rameses to Succoth, about six hundred thousand men on foot, besides children. A mixed multitude went up with them also, and flocks and herds—a great deal of livestock (Exod. 12:29-38).

Most of the teaching we hear on Exodus 12 focuses on the miracle God wrought for His people when He delivered them from more than four centuries of bondage. But as we dig deeper into this portion of Scripture, we uncover other valuable truths, beginning with the judgment that was executed upon Egypt.

There are basically two reasons for biblical judgment to be triggered. The first is sin, including disobedience or rebellion. The children of Israel were in bondage in Egypt for 430 years as a result of their sin of rebellion. One of the definitions of judgment is "to inflict a sentence," which is just what those four centuries of slavery represented.

Another definition of judgment is "to be set right." The second reason that judgment may be triggered is to set things right. In the case of the captive children of Israel, this is what happened when they were finally released from bondage.

God said, "I will pass through the land of Egypt on that night, and will strike all the firstborn in the land of Egypt, both man and beast; and against all the gods of Egypt I will execute judgment" (Exod. 12:12).

In essence, God was saying, "It's time for My people to leave; their sentence is over. I'm going to execute judgment on those who have kept them in bondage, and I'm going to set things right."

So, what, exactly, did setting things right entail? Exodus 12:36 says, "And the LORD had given the people favor in the sight of the Egyptians, so that they granted them what they requested. Thus they plundered the Egyptians." The *Amplified* translation says, "And they stripped the Egyptians [of those things]," referring to gold, silver and clothing.

Notice the two things that happened as a result of Israel's obedience: First, they experienced favor as they'd never known it before. Second, they experienced a restoration of all that had been stolen from them. Not only did these people get back what belonged to them, but God also saw to it that they got back what had belonged to their ancestors. They didn't walk out of captivity with just what belonged to their own generation; they walked out with what had belonged to previous generations as well. God indeed had set things right for the children of Israel, just as He had promised when He said to Abraham, "I will bless those who bless you, and I will curse him who curses you" (Gen. 12:3).

Earlier, we discussed Abraham's being an example for us, his spiritual seed, in that he left his country and his family in order to obtain the lifestyle of faith and favor that God had planned for him. Abraham was also an example for his natural seed, the children of Israel, who exercised their faith in the God of Abraham, Isaac and Jacob when they obeyed the words that God had given to Moses. They knew that Abraham had once been called to go to a place that he would receive as an inheritance, and they believed that what God had done for Abraham, He would do for them, too.

They could have chosen to remain in captivity, where they had become accustomed to the comfort of the familiar: the familiar culture, the familiar mindsets, and the familiar way of doing things. But they were willing to pay the price of obedience—which involved leaving the familiar behind—in order to obtain all that God had promised them.

As a result of their obedience to leave behind a life of captivity to the culture in which they had been born, God poured out His favor upon His people. As He led them out of Egypt, He went before them by day in a pillar of cloud and by night in a pillar of fire. He provided them with food to eat and water to drink. He led them across the sea on dry ground and then destroyed their enemies before their eyes. Although at times the lure of the familiar tugged at the Israelites and they desired to return to Egypt, ultimately the Lord led them into the land of promise, just as He had declared He would.

Because of our faith in Jesus Christ, we have been redeemed from the curse and are entitled to walk in the blessing and the favor of God. We can choose not to conform to our culture and the ways of thinking that have been passed on to us by former generations. We can renew our minds to the Word of God, leaving behind the mindset of mediocrity and believing instead that

God's favor will cause us to be blessed when we come in and when we go out. It will cause our enemies to flee before us, and it will make us the head and not the tail as God opens His good treasure to us to bless all the work of our hands.

Make the decision right now to pay the price of obedience. Once you do that, it won't be long before you begin to experience a higher level of God's favor manifesting in every area of your life.

6

CONSISTENT FAVOR REQUIRES CONSISTENT OBEDIENCE

In the more than 40 years since Carolyn and I first received a revelation of the favor of God and began walking and living in it, we have enjoyed a very blessed life—but that's not to say we've never faced adversity. Over the same 40 years, we have also experienced numerous attacks: attacks on our health, our family, our ministry and our finances—attacks just like everyone else in the Body of Christ experiences.

However, because we know that the favor of God is upon our lives, we are confident that if we do not give up under the pressure of the attack, our enemy will not triumph over us. We can say with David, "By this I know that thou favourest me, because mine enemy doth not triumph over me" (Ps. 41:11, *KJV*). We might get knocked down, but we don't believe in staying down. When we fall, we shall arise. Why? Because the favor of God is upon our lives.

Have you ever wondered why some people never seem to enter the flow of God's blessing and favor, while others appear to walk in it continuously? Why is that? Is God arbitrarily picking and choosing? Of course not. We are the ones who do the choosing. The Word of God is very clear about whom God intends to bless: all of mankind. God wants every person to experience His blessing and favor—but we must make the choice to receive what He offers.

After God had delivered the Israelites from slavery in Egypt, Joshua spoke these words to the people: "Now therefore, fear the LORD, serve Him in sincerity and in truth, and put away the gods which your fathers served on the other side of the River and in Egypt. Serve the LORD! And if it seems evil to you to serve the LORD, choose for yourselves this day whom you will serve, whether the gods which your fathers served that were on the other side of the River, or the gods of the Amorites, in whose land you dwell. But as for me and my house, we will serve the LORD" (Josh. 24:14-15). Just as deciding to set aside old mindsets is a choice we have to make, so is choosing to serve and obey the Lord. With the choice to serve Him come His blessing and favor.

The book of Proverbs provides us with both wisdom and instruction for successful living. I particularly like the way Proverbs 3 lays out the benefits of blessing and favor that come with choosing to serve the Lord:

> My son, do not forget my law, but let your heart keep my commands; for length of days and long life and peace they will add to you.

> Let not mercy and truth forsake you; bind them around your neck, write them on the tablet of your heart, and so find favor and high esteem in the sight of God and man.
>
> Trust in the LORD with all your heart, and lean not on your own understanding; in all your ways acknowledge Him, and He shall direct your paths.
>
> Do not be wise in your own eyes; fear the LORD and depart from evil. It will be health to your flesh, and strength to your bones.
>
> Honor the LORD with your possessions, and with the firstfruits of all your increase; so your barns will be filled with plenty, and your vats will overflow with new wine (Prov. 3:1-10).

As you can see, when we choose to be obedient to God's instruction, not only will we find favor and esteem in His sight and in the sight of man, but we can also expect that God will direct our paths, give us physical health and well-being, and bless us with material prosperity.

While God's favor and blessing have been freely given and made available to us through faith in Jesus Christ, not everyone will walk in that favor. As Proverbs 3 goes on to say, "The curse of the LORD is on the house of the wicked, but He blesses the home of the just" (Prov. 3:33).

Who are the wicked? When we think of wicked people, we usually think of evil, ungodly, nasty people—people you certainly wouldn't want hanging out at your house all the time. That's one form of wickedness—and one that the Bible certainly covers. But in the book of Matthew, we find a different application of the word "wicked."

As Jesus shares with His disciples what we have come to know as the parable of the talents, He talks about how the master entrusted a different number of talents to each of his three servants to invest while he was away on a journey. Two of the servants invested the talents wisely, doubling their master's resources. The master commended each of those two, saying, "Well done, good and faithful servant" (Matt. 25:23). But out of fear, the third servant buried the talent that had been entrusted to his care. When his master found out that this servant had produced nothing with what he'd been given, his response was: "You wicked and lazy servant . . . you ought to have deposited my money with the bankers, and at my coming I would have received back my own with interest" (vv. 26-27).

As we can see from this example, wickedness is not just evil or ungodliness. It can also be defined as being unfaithful. So when we read that the curse of the Lord is on the house of the wicked, what does the Bible mean by that?

First, let's look at the word "curse." In order to understand the concept of the curse correctly, let's remember the covenant God made with mankind when He created the first man and woman (see Gen. 1:28-30). Within that covenant He established His favor, His blessing, and everything they would need for living a fruitful life—provided that they chose to obey His instructions (see Gen. 2:16-17). But instead, they chose to disobey God, essentially committing high treason against Him (see Gen 3:1-7). As a result of their disobedience, the curse came upon all mankind (see Gen. 3:8-19). God never intended for His creation to experience this curse, but every act of disobedience carries consequences.

Proverbs 26:2 says, "Like a flitting sparrow, like a flying swallow, so a curse without cause shall not alight." The *New Living Translation* says that "an undeserved curse will not land on its intended victim." In other words, if you do not give the curse a cause, then it cannot land on your house.

The word "house" certainly pertains to a physical structure in which people live. But it also refers to the person or persons who live in the structure, as well as their possessions. That's where we get the word "household."

The *Amplified* translation of Proverbs 3:33 says, "The curse of the Lord is in and on the house of the wicked, but He declares blessed (joyful and favored with blessings) the home of the just and consistently righteous." As I said earlier, God doesn't go around picking certain people to bless and leaving out others. The choice to walk in the favor and blessing of God is ours.

In Deuteronomy 30:19, God says, "I call heaven and earth as witnesses today against you, that I have set before you life and death, blessing and cursing; therefore choose life, that both you and your descendants may live." God says He has two offers for us: life and blessing, or death and cursing. I like to say that He then gives us an inside tip: Choose life. Choose the blessing. But notice whose choice it is.

God does not make the decision for us; He just tells us it's a whole lot better if we choose life and blessing. That initial choice then leads to countless day-to-day choices. How we live our lives determines whether or not we experience the continuous flow of His favor and blessing.

GOD SAYS HE HAS TWO OFFERS FOR US: LIFE AND BLESSING, OR DEATH AND CURSING. I LIKE TO SAY THAT HE THEN GIVES US AN INSIDE TIP: CHOOSE LIFE.

My heart goes out to people who are struggling. It particularly grieves me to see so many of God's people just give up and choose to quit operating in the truths they have learned. Now, please understand that I am not being judgmental. It's just that over four decades, I've learned some things. I've made some mistakes, but I've gained insight from those mistakes. I've learned what brings God's favor to my house, and I know what keeps it away. My intention in sharing these truths with you is that you might experience God's favor operating in your life on a daily basis.

I believe three choices determine whether or not we walk in the favor of God that is available to us: obedience, consistency, and what we say.

Develop a Lifestyle of Obedience

Once again, when the Bible talks about the curse of the Lord, it's talking about the curse that comes through disobedience. When God laid out the choice of life or death, blessing or cursing, He made it clear that the curse can't touch those who are obedient to choose life. This is why it is so important that we develop a lifestyle of obedience.

As the Israelites were about to take possession of the Promised Land, Moses stressed the importance of being obedient to the commandments they had been given:

> Now this is the commandment, and these are the statutes and judgments which the LORD your God has commanded to teach you, that you may observe them in the land which you are crossing over to possess, that you may fear the LORD your God, to keep all His statutes and His commandments which I command you . . . all the days of your life, and that your days may be prolonged. . . . And these words which I command you today shall be in your heart. You shall teach them diligently to your children, and shall talk of them when you sit in your house, when you walk by the way, when you lie down, and when you rise up (Deut. 6:1-2,6-7).

What was Moses doing? He was sowing seeds for a lifestyle of obedience. He was creating a new mindset that would enable this nation of people to walk in the favor and blessing of God. But practicing obedience was the key.

Jesus Himself had to practice obedience. He said, "I do not seek My own will, but the will of the Father who sent Me" (John 5:30). Jesus' job was to do the will of the Father, and our job is to follow Jesus' example and do the same. Luke 6:46 records a very blunt question Jesus once posed: "But why do you call Me 'Lord, Lord,' and not do the things which I say?" When someone refers to Jesus as Lord, it's the same as calling Him Master. It means—or should mean—that person is totally submitted to Him, and that He has final authority in that person's life. So Jesus was asking, "Why are you calling Me Lord when you don't do what I say?" The *Amplified* translation says, "Why do you call Me, Lord, Lord, and do not [practice] what I tell you?"

I played lots of baseball when I was young, and I can tell you that our team spent more time practicing than we did actually playing the game. Practice was designed to get us to the point that we could excel at the sport. Whether or not we won the game, we'd have practice again the next day. If we won the championship at the end of one season, we'd start the next season with practice. I never told my coach, "Hey, I practiced all last year. We won the championship. I know how to do this, so I'll just skip practice and see you at the game." If I had been foolish enough to say that, he would have told me not to bother showing up for the game.

To return to Jesus' question, in essence, He was asking, "Why are you calling Me Lord if you're not practicing what I tell you?" In this context, we could define the word "practice" as "to apply repeatedly until it becomes a lifestyle." When we determine to develop lifestyles of obedience, it won't be long before we'll see the blessing and favor of God manifesting on our houses.

Baseball was a good teacher for me, but so was the military. In the Army, I learned not to question orders and not to make excuses. If you made a mistake, you didn't give your commanding officer an excuse—even if you thought the order you'd been given was the dumbest thing you'd ever heard. You just said, "No excuse, sir." That's the way you acted if you wanted to maintain right standing and not end up in the brig.

God is not going to hurt us if we mess up, but we can certainly hurt ourselves when we get out from under the umbrella of His protection that is established in our lives through our obedience. For this reason, Carolyn and I knew it was important to teach our children obedience from an early age.

GOD IS NOT GOING TO HURT US IF WE MESS UP, BUT WE CAN HURT OURSELVES WHEN WE GET OUT FROM UNDER THE UMBRELLA OF HIS PROTECTION.

When our girls were very young, I found the Scripture verse that says, "Children, obey your parents in all things, for this is well pleasing to the Lord" (Col. 3:20). One translation refers to children who obey quickly and quietly (see 1 Tim. 3:4, *TLB*). That was just what I was looking for. I went to my daughters and said, "From now on, this is the way you will obey your mother and dad: quickly and quietly. This means don't argue, don't hesitate, don't debate, and don't try to come up with a better idea."

I was so glad I'd found that Scripture, but when I'd finished laying it on my children, the Lord said to me, "That goes for you, too, sonny boy."

When we choose to enter into lifestyles of obedience to God's Word, we'll find that the blessing and favor of God will rest upon our houses, as we've already read in Proverbs 3:33: "He declares blessed (joyful and favored with blessings) the home of the just and consistently righteous" (*AMP*). I particularly like this translation of the verse, because it uses a word that other translations do not use. That word is "consistently."

This brings us to the second factor that determines the level of favor and blessing in our lives: consistency.

Consistency: The Missing Ingredient

I once stopped in the middle of a sermon and asked an elderly man in the church where I was preaching, "Sir, how long have you been in this church?"

His matter-of-fact answer was: "Thirty years."

"Really? Where'd you get saved?"

"In this church."

"So you've been in this church ever since you got saved," I said. "Let me ask you this: Does your pastor ever preach anything that you don't agree with?"

"Yes."

"And you're still here?"

"Yes."

So I asked him, "How can that be, if you don't agree with everything he preaches?"

"Well, when I went home and read the Bible for myself, I found out he was right." This man's consistency and faithfulness spoke volumes to me.

Unfortunately, he is an exception rather than the rule—I would even go so far as to say that inconsistency is a disease that afflicts the Body of Christ today. It's not unusual for a pastor to say something that people may not like. But instead of setting it aside for further study, as this man did, how do many people respond? "I'm out of here!" They lack consistency, or "stickability."

I've learned that most Christians are great starters—but not always great finishers. We get inspired and excited about the potential we have and the kind of life that is available to us through the Word of God, but we don't always demonstrate consistency in our attempts to achieve that lifestyle. My personal opinion is that consistency is the name of the game if we want a lifestyle marked by the blessing and favor of God.

Now, when it comes to being consistent, I'm not perfect, by any means. But one thing I am consistent about is being obedient to the Word of God. It's not something I do only occasionally; it's my life. I don't go to church on Sunday, hear a word and obey it one time, and then decide I don't want to be obedient anymore. That's not consistency.

So, what exactly is consistency? Let's look at some of the definitions of the word. "Consistency" means "firmness of character"; a consistent person is "resolute; non-compromising; persistent; free from distractions." Another way to put it is to say that being consistent is taking on the very nature of Jesus Christ. Hebrews 13:8 tells us that "Jesus Christ is the same yesterday, today, and forever." That's consistency.

Developing a lifestyle of consistent obedience requires us not only to delve into the Word of God, but also to do those things that we have learned. James put it this way: "But be doers of the word, and not hearers only, deceiving yourselves. For if anyone is a hearer of the word and not a doer, he is like a man observing his natural face in a mirror; for he observes himself, goes away, and immediately forgets what kind of man he was" (Jas. 1:22-24). In order to walk in the blessing and favor of God, we need to do what the Word tells us to do, and we need to do it every day of our lives. We need to keep the Word before us 24/7 and obey it consistently. This is how we open the door for God's blessing to be upon our houses.

Deuteronomy 6:11 tells us that our houses will be "full of all good things." A house that is full of all good things is a house that the blessing of the Lord is upon. Carolyn and I have just such a house. As a matter of fact, every time I pull up in front of my house, whether I've been gone for an hour or a month, I always say, "I wonder what blessed people live here?" And then I say, "We do!" Carolyn and I are the blessed people who live there. Our house is paid for, and everything in it is paid for. God said in Deuteronomy that He would bless us with houses, and that's just what He has done for Carolyn and me.

Because we practice consistent obedience, our house is blessed. It doesn't matter what's happening in anybody else's house; we will not be affected by the weather or the stock market or the economy or anything else that's going on in the world. The Word of God says that "the wicked are overthrown and are no more, but the house of the righteous will stand" (Prov. 12:7). Similarly, in Proverbs 14:11, we read that "the house of the wicked will be overthrown, but the tent of the upright will flourish." In other words, we can expect to achieve success and to prosper continuously, no matter what the conditions around us may be.

While the blessing of God on our houses will cause us to flourish, it does not ensure that we will never have to do any home maintenance. I'm not talking about repairing a roof or treating for termites. As challenging as these issues can be in the natural, I'm talking about something more sinister: strife. Jesus made this statement: "If a house is divided against itself, that house cannot stand" (Mark 3:25). Anytime a house is full of strife, there will be no blessing on that house. Why? Because "where envying and strife is, there is confusion and every evil work" (Jas. 3:16, *KJV*). In other words, the curse is operating in that house. God didn't put it there. It's there because the people in that house removed their umbrella of protection.

Strife is a blessing blocker. Strife opens the door for the curse. Anytime there is strife in a house, the blessing will not operate on a continuous basis. Carolyn and I learned years ago not to let strife get a foothold in our house. That's not to say that we've never had a disagreement, but the Bible says not to "let the sun go down on your wrath" (Eph. 4:26), so we are always quick to deal with our issues and quick to forgive.

STRIFE IS A BLESSING BLOCKER. ANYTIME THERE IS STRIFE IN A HOUSE, THE BLESSING WILL NOT OPERATE ON A CONTINUOUS BASIS.

The apostle Paul also said that we should not "give place to the devil" (Eph. 4:27), which means that we should not give the curse a legal right to land on our houses. One way we avoid making room for the curse is by removing strife, but more importantly, we must be deliberate about the words we speak.

Our Words Carry Great Power

Once, when I was teaching on the favor of God and the power of our words, someone asked me, "Brother Jerry, are you saying that it's actually possible to stop the favor of God from operating in my life because of the words I speak?"

"That's exactly what I'm saying," was my response.

You see, words have great power. The Bible says that "the worlds were framed by the word of God" (Heb. 11:3). The book of Genesis describes that process:

> Then God said, "Let there be light"; and there was light. . . .
>
> Then God said, "Let there be a firmament in the midst of the waters, and let it divide the waters from the waters." Thus God made the firmament. . . .
>
> Then God said, "Let the earth bring forth grass, the herb that yields seed, and the fruit tree that yields fruit according to its kind, whose seed is in itself, on the earth"; and it was so. . . .
>
> Then God said, "Let Us make man in Our image" (Gen. 1:3,6-7,11,26).

Everything that God created, including mankind, was created by His spoken words. "God said . . . and it was so." It is evident that God's words carry great power. Doesn't it make sense that if He created us in His own image and gave us dominion over all of His creation, then our words also carry great power?

Jesus taught about the importance of the words we speak. He said, "For by your words you will be justified, and by your words you will be condemned" (Matt. 12:37). He also said, as you may recall, "For assuredly, I say to you, whoever says to this mountain, 'Be removed and be cast into the sea,' and does not doubt in his heart, but believes that those things he says will be done, he will have whatever he says" (Mark 11:23). What we say matters, and I've learned that ensuring a continuous flow of God's favor and blessing in my life doesn't get any more basic than watching my mouth.

I remember how my life changed, years ago, when I discovered that "death and life are in the power of the tongue, and those who love it will eat its fruit" (Prov. 18:21). As I began to learn about the power of words, I realized that my words could actually make me or break me. I discovered that my words would either set me free or take me captive. That's when I began to change what was coming out of my mouth. I put a guard on my vocabulary.

When I went into the ministry in 1969, I still had a lot of debt from my automotive business. I'd not yet learned about the importance of declaring God's favor over my life. I felt a lot of pressure from the notices in the mail and the phone calls I was getting. I was an honest man, and I'd determined that everyone was going to get paid; I just didn't know how I was going to do it.

Knowing that Jesus said, "If two of you agree on earth concerning anything that they ask, it will be done for them" (Matt.18:19), Carolyn and I made a pact with each other. We decided that if one of us started talking negatively, the other one would do one of two things: either get up and walk away, ending the conversation, or say, "Okay, that's your confession, and I'm setting myself in agreement because all it takes is two for it to come to pass."

Changing the way we talked didn't happen overnight. There were times when Carolyn might say something like, "How are we ever going to pay these bills? We'll never get out of debt."

I'd respond with, "That's your confession, so I'll just set myself in agreement with it."

Then she would quickly say, "I pull down those words in Jesus' name."

Or I might get up one morning and declare, "Dear God, I'm sicker than a dog. I'm so sick."

Carolyn would say, "All right, that's your confession; I agree that you're sicker than a dog."

So I'd hasten to say, "No, I'm not sicker than a dog; I am healed." That's how we began to train each other to put a guard over our mouths.

Even today there are times when I am tempted to burst out with a negative confession, but I know that I can't afford to let down the guard I've put on my mouth. There's too much at stake where the favor of God is concerned. I'm so serious about this that if I have to put some duct tape across my mouth to keep from talking negatively, then that's what I'll do.

The crucial choices we've been talking about—establishing lifestyles of consistent obedience and watching the words of our mouths—are not unrelated. In Proverbs 4, we find this admonition: "Hear, my children, the instruction of a father, and give attention to know understanding; for I give you good doctrine: do not forsake my law" (vv. 1-2). This chapter goes on to describe the benefits of obedience and the consequences of disobedience. In verse 24 of the *King James* version, we're given the following key:

"Put away from thee a froward mouth, and perverse lips put far from thee."

Do you know what a froward mouth is? The simplest definition I can give you is this: A froward mouth is a disobedient mouth. A froward mouth says whatever it wants, based on how it feels, regardless of what the Scripture says. A froward mouth is a mouth that is not under control because the tongue is not under control. James talked about the importance of taming the tongue:

> If anyone does not stumble in word, he is a perfect man, able also to bridle the whole body. Indeed, we put bits in horses' mouths that they may obey us, and we turn their whole body. Look also at ships: although they are so large and are driven by fierce winds, they are turned by a very small rudder wherever the pilot desires. Even so the tongue is a little member and boasts great things.
>
> See how great a forest a little fire kindles! And the tongue is a fire, a world of iniquity. The tongue is so set among our members that it defiles the whole body, and sets on fire the course of nature; and it is set on fire by hell. For every kind of beast and bird, of reptile and creature of the sea, is tamed and has been tamed by mankind. But no man can tame the tongue. It is an unruly evil, full of deadly poison. With it we bless our God and Father, and with it we curse men, who have been made in the similitude of God. Out of the same mouth proceed blessing and cursing. My brethren, these things ought not to be so. Does a spring send forth fresh water and bitter from

> the same opening? Can a fig tree, my brethren, bear olives, or a grapevine bear figs? Thus no spring yields both salt water and fresh (Jas. 3:2-12).

James said the tongue is such an unruly member of the body that it can set on fire the course of nature. He said we can control horses and ships, but we can't control the tongue. You may be thinking, *Well, if we can't control our tongues, why are you telling me to watch my mouth?*

James was making the point that we can control horses and ships with the natural power of bits and rudders, but there is no natural power by which we can control the tongue. Controlling the tongue requires the supernatural power of God, and that power comes from the Word of God. We've got to fill our hearts with the Word, and then out of the abundance of the heart, the mouth will speak.

In chapter 2, we learned the importance of declaring the favor of God. We learned that there is a connection between our declaring the favor of God in our lives and our experiencing the manifestation of that favor. I've certainly found this to be true in my own life.

For a period of time, I didn't declare the favor of God as consistently as I had when I first took hold of this truth. As a result, I wasn't seeing the manifestations of God's favor as frequently as before. Something powerful happens when we release God's Word from our mouths. Job 22:28 says, "You will also declare a thing, and it will be established for you." In other words, when we use our mouths to declare the favor of God, He sees to it that

His favor is established in our lives and upon our houses. Once I again started declaring the favor of God on a consistent basis, miraculous things began happening on a more consistent basis.

GOD DESIRES THAT WE ENJOY THE BENEFITS OF A LIFE MARKED BY HIS FAVOR. BUT WALKING CONSISTENTLY IN THAT FAVOR REQUIRES THAT WE WALK IN CONSISTENT OBEDIENCE TO HIS WORD.

God desires that each and every one of us enjoy the benefits of a life marked by His favor. But walking consistently in that favor requires that we walk in consistent obedience to His Word, taking care to guard what comes out of our mouths and speak only words of life, blessing and favor.

For more than 40 years, I have made this my confession: *The favor of God is on me, the favor of God surrounds me, and the favor of God goes before me. I have access to the throne of divine favor, and in time of need that favor comes my way.* Won't you join me and make this your confession, too?

7

POSITIONED FOR FAVOR

I had heard the call of God when I was a boy, yet because preaching the gospel was not what I wanted to do, I had been running as hard and fast from that call as I possibly could. But deep down inside, although I wasn't willing to admit it, I knew that if I didn't surrender my life to God, I was going to be miserable no matter what level of success I achieved.

Finally, I got tired of running—and of merely existing. I wanted life. Real life. I knew that the only way I would ever experience that kind of life was in Christ. After decades of resistance (by this time I was a grown man who had been married for three years), I finally realized that I needed God, and I needed Him desperately. I knew that my life belonged to Him. So at three o'clock on a cold February morning in 1969, I lifted my hands and said, "Lord, I don't know if You still want me or not. I've been running from You all these years, but if You still want me, here I am."

Then I added, "I think it's important that I let You know what a failure You're getting." As if He didn't know.

But before I could say another thing, I heard Him speak these words to me: "Don't worry about it, son. I'm a master at making champions out of failures."

From the moment that I surrendered my life to Him—and I'm not talking about a month or two later, but from that very moment—I just couldn't get enough of God. All of a sudden, I wanted to devour the Bible that Carolyn had given me several years earlier. When I opened my business, she brought it to my office, because she wanted me to have a Bible at work. As soon as she had left, I hid it. I didn't want any of my clients seeing a Bible in my office. But after I surrendered to God, I went looking for that Bible. I finally found it under all of my paint and parts catalogs in my desk. I started reading it and couldn't get enough of it. Even though I was scripturally illiterate, I began to study that Bible, and I soon discovered that God was a whole lot better than what I'd heard about Him.

Growing up, I heard people say, "You'd better watch out, or God is going to get you." I heard that so much that I got the idea God was mean. But then I found out that God is love. I found out that He loved *me*, and that He had an awesome plan for my life. I found out that He favored me, and that His favor was for a lifetime. I hadn't discovered yet that I could have a continuous flow of favor and blessing in my life, because I didn't know that bestowing continuous favor and blessing on His children was the will of God.

I can't expect God to give me something that is not His will. Kenneth Hagin used to say that faith operates where there is the known will of God. In other words, our faith will operate at its highest level when we know the will of God. For instance, if I'm not sure that it's God's will to heal me, then obviously I'm not going to have strong faith where healing is concerned. If I don't know that it's God's will to prosper me, then I'll struggle when it comes to asking Him for prosperity.

So, I had to establish from the Word of God that it is His will for me to experience a continuous, uninterrupted flow of favor and blessing—no matter what the conditions and circumstances are in the natural.

We saw in chapter 3 that the first thing God did after creating man and woman was to pronounce a blessing over them: "Then God blessed them, and God said to them, 'Be fruitful and multiply; fill the earth and subdue it; have dominion over the fish of the sea, over the birds of the air, and over every living thing that moves on the earth'" (Gen. 1:28). The Bible doesn't say that God blessed them for a season or for a short period of time or for a dispensation. Genesis (which means "beginning") is a revelation of God's will for mankind—and that will was for continuous blessing and favor.

We know that Adam blew it, but God's intent for mankind to experience continuous favor and blessing didn't change. The first thing God did when He began dealing with Noah was to bless him in the same way He had blessed Adam and Eve: "So God blessed Noah and his sons, and said to them: 'Be fruitful and multiply, and fill the earth'" (Gen. 9:1).

We also know that the blessing conferred upon Abraham by God encompasses his natural progeny, meaning Isaac, Jacob and their descendants, and also his spiritual progeny, which includes you and me. God's blessing and favor will work in our lives today just as it worked for those whose stories we read about in the Bible. The fact that God's blessing and favor have been made available to us on a continuous basis is now firmly established for Carolyn and me, and our faith in the veracity of the Word of God is unwavering.

GOD'S BLESSING AND FAVOR WILL WORK IN OUR LIVES TODAY JUST AS IT WORKED FOR THOSE WHOSE STORIES WE READ ABOUT IN THE BIBLE.

Carolyn and I have known each other for nearly our whole lives. We met when I was 11 and she was 9, and we grew up on the same street. We went to school together, and to me she was always "the little girl down the street"—that is, until I came home after being away for a while at college. I hadn't seen her for two years, and as soon as I laid eyes on her, I noticed that she had certainly changed. We fell in love and were married in 1966. We're still in love today.

Now, we have a saying here in Texas: "You dance with the one that brung you." This means you don't go to a party with someone and then spend your time dancing with someone else. Carolyn and I have been dancing only with each other, so to speak, for most of our lives. We've been dancing with the Word of God since we fell in love with it in 1969. I'm not looking for another woman, and I'm not looking for another message, either.

The favor of God has been part of my life and ministry for more than 40 years. Although God's favor is available to me on a continuous basis, I've learned that there are three things I must do in order to position myself to experience that favor continuously.

I must be engaged in a continuous pursuit of God.

I must continuously approach God with a right motive.

I must maintain a right attitude on a continuous basis.

The Continuous Pursuit of God

God has an awesome plan for each and every one of us. But it begins with our pursuit of Him. The Bible says, "Draw near to God and He will draw near to you" (Jas. 4:8). God is never pushy. He invites us to take the first step.

I've discovered that when we take that first step, God is always there for those who are hungry for Him. Matthew 5:6 tells us, "Blessed are those who hunger and thirst for righteousness, for they shall be filled."

I believe there is something fresh taking place in our midst right now. I see people all over this country who hunger and thirst for God like never before. You know, an uncertain economy has a way of driving people to God. When the government isn't working as it should, people begin looking for answers elsewhere—and many of them turn to God.

I believe there is a call from heaven for God's people to begin a fresh pursuit of Him. Pursuing God is the only answer to the issues we face in life, regardless of whether the economy is good or bad. How do I know this? Because the Bible says, "Those who seek the LORD shall not lack any good thing" (Ps. 34:10).

Seeking the Lord is not a one-time experience; it is a progressive effort. And I can attest to the fact that those who continuously seek Him will lack nothing. Carolyn and I determined years ago that we were going to seek God with all that was within us—not just in the bad times, but all of the time, uninterrupted. God has honored that decision. His blessing and favor have flowed continuously in our life and ministry for more than 40 years—and what He's done for us, He will do for anyone. The Word tells us that God is not a respecter of persons (see Acts 10:34).

Moses spoke these words to God's people: "You shall love the LORD your God with all your heart, with all your soul, and with all your strength" (Deut. 6:5). The *Amplified* translation says to love Him "with your entire being." When we love God like this, we will never stop pursuing Him. Our attitude will be: *I can't get enough of God.*

This is precisely the attitude the apostle Paul had when he penned his letter to the believers in Philippi. Most theologians agree that Paul had been walking with the Lord for some 30 years at that time. He had been shipwrecked, imprisoned, bitten by a snake, beaten, and nearly stoned to death, but God had delivered him each time. After three decades of relationship with God, Paul wrote, "I have suffered the loss of all things, and count them as rubbish . . . that I may know Him" (Phil. 3:8,10). Paul had known God intimately for 30 years, but he wanted to know Him more.

Do you suppose that Paul's hunger for God was the reason God always showed up in the worst imaginable circumstances? Paul didn't run *from* God in his times of adversity. He ran *to* God.

As Christians, the worst mistake we can make when we're going through difficult times is to run from God. In bad times, it's always best to run to Him—the way a young boy named Uzziah did following the death of his father, Amaziah, king of Judah:

> Uzziah was sixteen years old when he became king, and he reigned fifty-two years in Jerusalem. His mother's name was Jecholiah of Jerusalem. And he did what was right in the sight of the LORD, according to all that his father Amaziah had done. He sought God in the days of Zechariah, who had understanding in the visions of God; and as long as he sought the LORD, God made him prosper (2 Chron. 26:3-5).

Notice the final part of this passage: "as long as he sought the LORD, God made him prosper." The condition was that he would prosper as long as he sought the Lord. In other words, if Uzziah ever stopped pursuing the Lord, then he himself would break the cycle of prosperity.

God put the ball in Uzziah's court, so to speak, and the same is true for us today. The ball is in our court. God is saying, "If you want what I originally intended for your life, which is a continuous flow of my favor and blessing, all you have to do is pursue me on a continuous basis." The moment we stop pursuing God, we stop the cycle of favor and blessing, and we open ourselves up to Satan, whose purpose is to steal, kill and destroy—if we allow it.

Jesus addressed the ways Satan works in the lives of believers when He explained the parable of the sower. Speaking of those believers represented by the seed that grew up among the thorns, Jesus said, "They are the ones who hear the word, and the cares of this world . . . choke the word, and it becomes unfruitful" (Mark 4:18-19). The *Amplified* translation says that this seed is choked not only by "the cares and anxieties of the world" but also by "the distractions of the age."

I don't think there's ever been a time when we've had more distractions than we have right now. In this age of technology, there is so much out there vying for our time and attention: television, movies, the Internet, and all the latest gadgets. Understand that I'm not being critical of these things; they are a fact of life in our fast-paced, high-tech world. In fact, the same technology that often distracts us can also prove to be a blessing.

For instance, I was recently introduced to my first iPad. This is an amazing piece of technology that allows me to take my entire library of faith material with me wherever I go. I used to carry five suitcases with me when I went somewhere to preach; that's how much reference material I had. Now I can carry all of that information in one hand.

I've also had my staff download other preachers' messages onto my iPod so that I can listen to them when I travel. On a recent 21-hour flight to Tanzania, I listened to sermons by John Osteen, T.L. Osborn, Oral Roberts, Kenneth Hagin and Kenneth Copeland. Listening to these messages back to back was a wonderful experience, provided by a little device that fit in my shirt pocket.

My point is this: With the technology available to us today, there is absolutely no excuse for the Body of Christ not to pursue God on a continuous basis.

When God told Joshua, "This Book of the Law shall not depart from your mouth, but you shall meditate in it day and night" (Josh. 1:8), He was saying, "If you want a continuous flow of My blessing and favor in your life, then make this a daily encounter." Pursuing God is not something we are to do only on Sunday or once a year at a convention. We are to seek Him continuously.

THOSE WHO PURSUE GOD ON A CONTINUOUS BASIS WILL EXPERIENCE A CONTINUOUS FLOW OF HIS FAVOR AND BLESSING.

Those who pursue God on a continuous basis will experience a continuous flow of His favor and blessing—in both good times and bad.

Approach God with a Right Motive

The second thing we can do to position ourselves for a continuous flow of God's favor and blessing is always to approach God with a right motive.

Speaking through the prophet Jeremiah, the Lord said, "I the Lord search the heart, I try the reins, even to give every man according to his ways, and according to the fruit of his doings" (Jer. 17:10, *KJV*). When God says, "I try the reins," what does that mean?

This same passage in *THE MESSAGE* reads, "I get to the root of things." According to the *New Living Translation*, God "examine[s] secret motives." So we can see that with God, motive matters.

Therefore, we have to ask ourselves, *Why do I want a continuous flow of God's favor and blessing in my life?* We've certainly established that it is God's will for us, but why do we want blessing and favor?

If our desire is to be blessed just so we can have everything we've ever wanted, then it's a pretty shallow desire. As a matter of fact, this motive is not even scriptural. Nor is the desire to be blessed so that we can brag about what we have. God is not against our having the things we want, but He is concerned with our motives for wanting them.

To make sure our motives line up with God's purpose for bestowing His favor and blessing in the first place, let's look again to the book of Genesis and what God said to Abraham: "I will make you a great nation; I will bless you and make your name great; and you shall be a blessing" (Gen. 12:2).

So, if we desire the blessing of Abraham, we've also got to accept the call of Abraham—and that call is to be a blessing to others. What does it mean to be a blessing? In modern-day language, it means to be a distributor. To have a right motive in our pursuit of continuous blessing and favor, we must understand that we are to be distributors of that blessing and favor. Our job is to receive God's blessing and favor and then to further His kingdom by helping other people along the way.

When Carolyn and I first got the revelation of the favor of God, we didn't own much of anything. But we decided that when the manifestation of the blessing began to flow in our lives, we would become a distribution center. We said, "We are blessed to be a blessing, so we won't hoard it for ourselves." We kept in mind the words of James: "You ask and do not receive, because you ask amiss, that you may spend it on your pleasures" (Jas. 4:3). The *New International Version* puts it this way: "When you ask, you do not receive, because you ask with wrong motives, that you may spend what you get on your pleasures."

It didn't happen overnight, but those blessings did begin to flow in our lives—and as they did, we kept our word to God that we would be a distribution center. To this day, our greatest monthly outlay of money is not a mortgage payment or a car note. It's our giving. More money goes out of our personal income to help other people than for any other expense in our life. We kept our word to God, and He kept His word to us. We are blessed to be a blessing; that's our motive.

God doesn't mind if we're wealthy, as long as we have a right motive. I like to think of wealth as "money with a mission" or "prosperity with a purpose." Jesus said that a person's life does not consist of possessions. God doesn't measure wealth by what we possess; rather, He measures it by what we give away. For example, consider the story of Jesus' encounter with the rich young ruler:

> Now a certain ruler asked Him, saying, "Good Teacher, what shall I do to inherit eternal life?"
>
> So Jesus said to him, "Why do you call Me good? No one is good but One, that is, God. You know the commandments: 'Do not commit adultery,' 'Do not murder,' 'Do not steal,' 'Do not bear false witness,' 'Honor your father and your mother.' "
>
> And he said, "All these things I have kept from my youth."

> So when Jesus heard these things, He said to him, "You still lack one thing. Sell all that you have and distribute to the poor, and you will have treasure in heaven; and come, follow Me."
>
> But when he heard this, he became very sorrowful, for he was very rich (Luke 18:18-23).

Notice that the young man told Jesus he'd kept God's commandments from his youth. That's why he was wealthy. But when he pursued Jesus and sought the truth about eternal life, he ended up walking away from that truth grieved—because he had great possessions.

Let's read between the lines here: Not only did the rich young ruler have great possessions, but those possessions also had him. How do we know if something has us? The answer is: if we can't give it away. In other words, if we can't sow something that God has given to us, then we don't have it—it has us.

In Paul's second letter to the Corinthians, he wrote about sowing, reaping and motives of the heart. I particularly like the way the *Amplified Bible* translates what Paul said:

> [Remember] this: he who sows sparingly and grudgingly will also reap sparingly and grudgingly, and he who sows generously [that blessings may come to someone] will also reap generously and with blessings.
>
> Let each one [give] as he has made up his own mind and purposed in his heart, not reluctantly or sorrowfully or under compulsion, for God loves (He takes pleasure

> in, prizes above other things, and is unwilling to abandon or to do without) a cheerful (joyous, "prompt to do it") giver [whose heart is in his giving].
>
> And God is able to make all grace (every favor and earthly blessing) come to you in abundance, so that you may always and under all circumstances and whatever the need be self-sufficient [possessing enough to require no aid or support and furnished in abundance for every good work and charitable donation].
>
> As it is written, He [the benevolent person] scatters abroad; He gives to the poor; His deeds of justice and goodness and kindness and benevolence will go on and endure forever!
>
> And [God] Who provides seed for the sower and bread for eating will also provide and multiply your [resources for] sowing and increase the fruits of your righteousness [which manifests itself in active goodness, kindness, and charity].
>
> Thus you will be enriched in all things and in every way, so that you can be generous, and [your generosity as it is] administered by us will bring forth thanksgiving to God (2 Cor. 9:6-11).

Notice that Paul said God would provide and multiply your resources for sowing. When was the last time you asked God not just to multiply your resources, but to multiply your resources for *sowing*? Paul understood the impact that an individual's motive has on receiving God's favor and blessing. He said, "Let him who stole steal no longer, but rather let him labor, working with his hands what is good, that he may have something to give him who has need" (Eph. 4:28).

Paul exhorts us to look at our jobs with a different perspective. The reason we have our work is not just to make a living; it's also God's way of providing us with seed for sowing.

When we develop a mindset of "I live to give," then we know that we have the right motive when we approach God. When we declare, "Let there be a continuous flow of favor and blessing in my life," God also knows that the motive of our hearts is right.

WHEN WE DECLARE, "LET THERE BE A CONTINUOUS FLOW OF FAVOR AND BLESSING IN MY LIFE," GOD ALSO KNOWS THAT THE MOTIVE OF OUR HEARTS IS RIGHT.

Carolyn and I live to give, and I will tell you that giving has become one of our greatest joys in life. God has blessed us because our motive is right—and what He's done for us, He will most certainly do for anyone whose heart is pure before Him.

Maintaining a Right Attitude

I've always been somewhat of a perfectionist, in that I'm methodical and meticulous. I like to do things correctly, and I like everything to be in its place. My daughters have told me, "Daddy, you could come home after being gone for a year, and you'd know if we'd used one of your pencils." When carried to the extreme, this kind of attention to detail can become a stumbling block. But when the Holy Spirit sanctifies it, it can be developed into what I like to call "an attitude of excellence."

In order to position ourselves to receive and operate in the favor of God, we must develop and maintain an attitude of excellence. We can actually hinder God's favor from manifesting to the fullest in our lives if we have the attitude that we will do just enough to get by and only meet the minimum requirements set before us.

During my first year in college, I needed a job, and I was thrilled when the engineering firm that was designing the Louisiana portion of Interstate 20 hired me as a draftsman. My job was to examine aerial photos under a magnifying glass to determine which houses and commercial properties would need to be removed to accommodate the new highway.

My superiors at this firm were all college graduates, many from the school I was attending, and I naturally wanted to provide the best service I could for them. Sometimes I couldn't clearly identify a structure from a photo, and because I didn't want to remove anything unnecessarily, I'd go to my supervisor and ask, "What do you think about this?"

Invariably he'd answer, "Well, just go ahead and take it out; it's close enough for government work."

I heard that phrase often enough over the course of my employment with the firm that it planted a seed in me. At some point, I stopped striving for excellence and developed a "that's good enough" attitude. It wasn't long before that attitude showed up in everything I did. I expended the least amount of effort required on every task and did anything I could to take the easy way out. Simply put, I got sloppy.

I'm happy to say that once I realized what had happened, I didn't let that attitude root itself any deeper in me. But the point I want to make is this: As Christians, we can't go around with a "that's good enough" attitude and always be looking for shortcuts in our walks of faith.

Proverbs 11:3 says, "The integrity of the upright will guide them," and verse 27 says, "He who earnestly seeks good finds favor." In other words, if we want to position ourselves to receive God's favor, then we must be diligent to maintain an attitude of excellence in everything we do.

Now, I'm not saying that God wants us to be perfectionists, but we must certainly guard against a "that's good enough" attitude carrying over into our spiritual lives. If that happens, we won't pray as consistently as we should, we won't fast, and we may get to the point that we do not want to listen to the Word. The Bible says, "He who despises the word will be destroyed, but he who fears the commandment will be rewarded. The law of the wise is a fountain of life, to turn one away from the snares of death. Good understanding gains favor" (Prov. 13:13-15).

God wants to pour out His favor—He wants to manifest it in our lives—but it will not come until we have the right attitude. We need to seek and then *expect* the favor of God. The young shepherd, David, who had slain both a lion and a bear that had attacked his father's flock of sheep, had already come to expect the favor of God when he went to visit his brothers in Saul's army.

The troops were engaged in a battle with the Philistines, and when David arrived, he found the entire army, including King Saul, in complete and total fear of the Philistine champion, Goliath. Their attitude was that they were already defeated.

> Then David said to Saul, "Let no man's heart fail because of him; your servant will go and fight with this Philistine."
>
> And Saul said to David, "You are not able to go against this Philistine to fight with him; for you are a youth, and he a man of war from his youth."
>
> But David said to Saul, "Your servant used to keep his father's sheep, and when a lion or a bear came and took a lamb out of the flock, I went out after it and struck it, and delivered the lamb from its mouth; and when it arose against me, I caught it by its beard, and struck and killed it. Your servant has killed both lion and bear; and this uncircumcised Philistine will be like one of them, seeing he has defied the armies of the living God." Moreover David said, "The LORD, who delivered me from the paw of the lion and from the paw of the bear, He will deliver me from the hand of this Philistine."
>
> And Saul said to David, "Go, and the LORD be with you!" . . .
>
> So it was, when the Philistine arose and came and drew near to meet David, that David hurried and ran toward the army to meet the Philistine. Then David put his hand in his bag and took out a stone; and he slung it and struck the Philistine in his forehead, so that the stone sank into

> his forehead, and he fell on his face to the earth. So David prevailed over the Philistine with a sling and a stone, and struck the Philistine and killed him. But there was no sword in the hand of David. Therefore David ran and stood over the Philistine, took his sword and drew it out of its sheath and killed him, and cut off his head with it.
>
> And when the Philistines saw that their champion was dead, they fled (1 Sam. 17:32-37,48-51).

What I want you to notice in this story is the stark difference in attitudes displayed by Saul and the boy David. While Saul saw Goliath as a man who was too big to kill, David saw the very same man as someone who was too big to miss. David looked at the giant and said, "There's no way I can miss that guy. He's so big, I know I can get him." That's exactly what David did, despite the fact that he was the youngest and smallest of his father's sons.

When I started playing Little League baseball at the age of nine, I was smaller than the other boys. The first day we all showed up to play—which was the day they determined who would be on the team—the coach said, "You boys line up, and I'm gong to walk in front of you. If I tap you on the shoulder, you come stand behind me. That means you made the team. If I don't tap you on the shoulder, you didn't make the team."

I was shaking in my shoes, waiting to see if I would be chosen. I knew that although I was small, I could play as well as—or even better than—most of the boys in line. But the coach didn't know that. When he tapped the two boys on either side of me, it was all I could do to keep from crying. After he had finished selecting the team, I went over to him and asked why I didn't make it. He said, "Son, you're too little."

At first I was devastated. But as it turned out, so many boys had come out wanting to play that another team was formed, and I ended up being the pitcher of that second team. We had a great season that year, and our team made it to the championship tournament. The best part of the experience was that the team we defeated for the Little League championship was the original team that had rejected me.

I'm so glad God doesn't see us the way the world sees us. He didn't look at me and say, "Sorry, little Jerry, I can't use you." The truth is, God chose me, and He chose you, because He wants to set us apart and make us distinct from the world. He wants to pour out His favor on us so that we can be ambassadors for His kingdom and touch the lives of others.

GOD CHOSE ME, AND HE CHOSE YOU, BECAUSE HE WANTS TO SET US APART AND MAKE US DISTINCT FROM THE WORLD.

When I think about an ambassador, I think of someone who is highly favored; I think of a person who routinely receives preferential treatment. Ambassadors who represent their nations often ride in big cars with flags on the fenders and are escorted and honored everywhere they go. That's how ambassadors expect to be treated. Being an ambassador in the kingdom of God brings even greater favor. We're not talking about merely representing the United States, or Canada, or Nigeria. We've been chosen to represent a kingdom that cannot be shaken. We represent the kingdom of the Most High God.

Dr. T.L. Osborn has been an ambassador for God for more than 60 years. He has conducted mass-miracle crusades all over the world and has probably led more people to Jesus than any other man alive today. I love to watch him, because he walks and talks like a prince. When he comes into a room, the presence that surrounds him identifies him as an ambassador of the kingdom of God—and as one who is highly favored.

The same is true for you and for me. God has not handpicked us because of our own doing, or because of our goodness or our great works. We've been chosen because of the goodness of Jesus—because of the work He did in our behalf at Calvary.

We have been made righteous because of Jesus; therefore, we can fully expect the favor of God to be poured out upon our lives as we continue to pursue God with right motives and a right attitude.

8

TEN BENEFITS OF WALKING IN GOD'S FAVOR

The dealership had told me up front how much it would cost to repair Carolyn's car, but the total on the invoice they presented to me was about half the amount they had quoted. When I pointed out the discrepancy, the service manager said, "We know it, Mr. Savelle, but you've been a good customer for so many years that the boss said to give you a 50 percent discount."

I thanked the man, smiled, and said, "That's the favor of God."

I always make it known that the favor of God operates in my life, but a lot of people still mistake His favor for luck. I can't tell you the number of times I've been told, "Jerry Savelle, you're the luckiest man I've ever seen."

I always reply, "It's not luck. It's the favor of God."

One time I was ready to fly home from London, and they didn't have a seat in the section where I wanted to sit. I didn't want to wind up in the only seat left, way back there by the toilet. So I started confessing the favor of God all the way to London

Heathrow. As my director for the U.K. ministry office drove me to the airport, I kept saying, "Geoff, I've got favor. I believe favor is going to open some doors and change some things when I get to the airport."

We walked right up to the check-in counter, and I told the agent my flight number. She went to the computer to make sure I was confirmed. Then she said, completely out of the blue, "I have the authority to upgrade."

I said, "That's wonderful to know."

"We had a cancellation and I'd like to put you in first class, if you don't mind."

I told her, "That's the favor of God."

"The what?"

"That's the favor of God." When I turned around to smile at Geoff, he was just shaking his head.

"You beat anything I've ever seen," he said. "I've never known anybody to have favor like you."

I said goodbye to Geoff, boarded the plane, and took the aisle seat on the front row, where I really like to sit. One of the flight attendants looked at me and said, "Oh my goodness–you're Jerry Savelle."

"Yes, ma'am."

"I've got one of your books in my purse," she said. "As soon as I get through serving these people, I'm going to come back and have you autograph it."

"I'd be happy to," I told her.

In a little while, the captain came out of the cockpit and said, "I don't believe it. Jerry Savelle."

"Yes, sir."

"I've been listening to your messages and reading your books for years. I'm going to tell the co-pilot to take over, and then I'll be back in a few moments. I want to talk to you."

It wasn't long before four flight attendants and the captain were sitting on the floor listening to me talk, every one of them wanting me to autograph books. After about 20 minutes, they thanked me and said, "We've got to get to work."

The whole time this was happening, the guy sitting next to me hadn't said a word. But as soon as the crew went back to work, he said, "I don't know who you are, and I don't know what you do, but I ain't had no service since you got on this airplane!"

I laughed and told him, "It's the favor of God."

If the favor of God will work to our benefit in little things like getting a seat on an airplane, what will it do when we're going through a financial crisis? What will it do when the world says, "No, no, no. You're not going to sell your house" or "You're not going to have this or that"?

The favor of God has the power to completely transform our lives. Let's go to the Bible and take a look at 10 specific benefits afforded to us when we walk in it.

Benefit #1: We Will Experience Supernatural Increase and Promotion

In chapter 2, we saw how the favor of God altered the destiny of Joseph, who was sold into slavery in Egypt by his own brothers. Because God's favor was upon him, he was placed in charge of everything that his master possessed—and the Lord blessed the house of the Egyptian for Joseph's sake.

Later, when Joseph was imprisoned after being falsely accused, he found favor with the keeper of the prison and was put in charge of the prisoners. But Joseph's story doesn't end there. Because God had given him the ability to interpret dreams, he was brought before Pharaoh.

> Then Pharaoh said to Joseph, "Inasmuch as God has shown you all this, there is no one as discerning and wise as you. You shall be over my house, and all my people shall be ruled according to your word; only in regard to the throne will I be greater than you." And Pharaoh said to Joseph, "See, I have set you over all the land of Egypt" (Gen. 41:39-41).

The favor of God most certainly altered the destiny of Joseph. It brought supernatural increase and promotion into his life, and it will do the same for you and for me.

Benefit #2:
We Will Experience the Restoration of Everything the enemy Has Stolen

We've learned that one of the definitions of the word "judgment" is "to be set right." God's people had been captives in Egypt for 430 years when He spoke these words to Moses:

> Go and gather the elders of Israel together, and say to them, "The Lord God of your fathers, the God of Abraham, of Isaac, and of Jacob, appeared to me, saying, 'I have surely vis-

> ited you and seen what is done to you in Egypt; and I have said I will bring you up out of the affliction of Egypt to the land of the Canaanites and the Hittites and the Amorites and the Perizzites and the Hivites and the Jebusites, to a land flowing with milk and honey.'" . . .
>
> And I will give this people favor in the sight of the Egyptians; and it shall be, when you go, that you shall not go empty-handed. But every woman shall ask of her neighbor, namely, of her who dwells near her house, articles of silver, articles of gold, and clothing; and you shall put them on your sons and on your daughters. So you shall plunder the Egyptians (Exod. 3:16-17,21-22).

God didn't intend for His people to walk out of captivity empty-handed. That's why He said they would "plunder" the Egyptians, which means "to spoil, to recover, to rescue, and to snatch away." But notice that the people had a part to play in this restoration; they had to put a demand on God's favor by *asking* for those things that God had promised them.

GOD DIDN'T INTEND FOR HIS PEOPLE TO WALK OUT OF CAPTIVITY EMPTY-HANDED. THAT'S WHY HE SAID THEY WOULD "PLUNDER" THE EGYPTIANS.

We, too, can put a demand on favor by making this declaration: "The favor of God will restore to me everything that the enemy has stolen!"

Benefit #3:
We Will Receive Honor—Even in the Midst of Our Adversaries

As a result of the ninth plague released against Egypt, the land experienced three days of what the Bible describes as "darkness which may even be felt" (Exod. 10:21). Yet the children of Israel had light in their dwellings throughout those three days. Just before God brought the tenth and final plague against Egypt, He spoke again to Moses:

> And the LORD said to Moses, "I will bring one more plague on Pharaoh and on Egypt. Afterward he will let you go from here. When he lets you go, he will surely drive you out of here altogether." . . . And the LORD gave the people favor in the sight of the Egyptians. Moreover the man Moses was very great in the land of Egypt, in the sight of Pharaoh's servants and in the sight of the people (Exod. 11:1,3).

Perhaps the most widely recognized of the psalms is Psalm 23. We have all read these words penned by David: "You prepare a table before me in the presence of my enemies" (Ps. 23:5). David was not the first person to experience honor in the presence of his enemies. He may have been inspired by the story of what God did for Moses and the Israelites.

God has said, "I am the LORD, I do not change" (Mal. 3:6); therefore, we know that what He has done for Moses and for David, He will most certainly do for us. His favor will bring us honor in the midst of our adversaries.

Benefit #4:
We Will Increase in Assets, Especially in the Area of Land and Real Estate

I have learned in my own life and ministry that as I confess that the favor of God goes before me and brings real estate into my possession, that is precisely what happens.

The same was true for God's people in biblical times. Following the death of Moses, God told Joshua to arise and take the people across the Jordan into the land He was giving them. He said, "Every place that the sole of your foot will tread upon I have given you, as I said to Moses" (Josh. 1:3). Just as God had promised, He delivered the land and assets into the Israelites' hands—and they didn't have to fight for it.

> I sent the hornet before you which drove them out from before you also, the two kings of the Amorites, but not with your sword or with your bow. I have given you a land for which you did not labor, and cities which you did not build, and you dwell in them; you eat of the vineyards and olive groves which you did not plant (Josh. 24:12-13).

We read in an earlier chapter that as Moses blessed the tribe of Naphtali with God's favor, he made the following declaration: "O Naphtali, satisfied with favor, and full of the blessing of the Lord, possess the west and the south" (Deut. 33:23).

I'm telling you, when we declare that God's favor will manifest as an increase in land and real estate, it happens. And guess what? We don't have to pay the world's price for it, either.

Benefit #5:
We Will Experience Great Victories in the Face of Long Odds

One of the things I've come to understand about walking in the favor of God is that the more impossible the battle looks, the more easily the victory will come. To return to the account of God's people entering the Promised Land, the Bible says of the armies gathered against Israel:

> And they went out, they and all their hosts with them, much people, even as the sand that is upon the sea shore in multitude, with horses and chariots very many. . . .
>
> And the LORD said unto Joshua, Be not afraid because of them: for tomorrow about this time will I deliver them up all slain before Israel. . . .
>
> So Joshua came, and all the people of war with him, against them . . . and they fell upon them.
>
> And the LORD delivered them into the hand of Israel. . . .
>
> For it was of the LORD to harden their hearts, that they should come against Israel in battle, that he might destroy them utterly, and that they might have no favour, but that he might destroy them, as the LORD commanded Moses (Josh. 11:4,6-8,20, *KJV*).

Although the enemy armies surrounding the Israelites were a multitude that possessed countless horses, chariots and, presumably, vast weapons of war, there was one thing that they did not possess: *favor*. When the favor of God is upon us, we can expect to experience great victories in the midst of the most daunting odds.

WHEN THE FAVOR OF GOD IS UPON US, WE CAN EXPECT TO EXPERIENCE GREAT VICTORIES IN THE MIDST OF THE MOST DAUNTING ODDS.

Benefit #6:
We Will Receive Recognition, Even When We Are the Least Likely to Be Selected

Many of us, at one time or another, have worked our hearts out, yet have not received the slightest appreciation or recognition. But when the favor of God shows up, that's when your situation will change. That's when you will get a promotion even though you seem to be the one least likely to receive it. This happened more than once in the life of David.

As a boy, David was the youngest and the smallest of the sons of Jesse, from among whom the prophet Samuel was to anoint a new king. When Jesse presented his sons to the old prophet, at first he didn't even include David. But when the young boy finally arrived, the Lord said to Samuel, "Arise, anoint him; for this is the one!" (1 Sam. 16:12).

David then went back to tending his father's sheep, but it wasn't long before Saul, the reigning king, sought him out:

> Therefore Saul sent messengers to Jesse, and said, "Send me your son David, who is with the sheep." And Jesse

> took a donkey loaded with bread, a skin of wine, and a young goat, and sent them by his son David to Saul. So David came to Saul and stood before him. And he loved him greatly, and he became his armorbearer. Then Saul sent to Jesse, saying, "Please let David stand before me, for he has found favor in my sight" (1 Sam. 16:19-22).

When the favor of God is upon us, we *will* be recognized. We don't have to go around telling others about it; instead, we can confess that favor to ourselves and praise God for it. When we do, it won't be long before we receive recognition—even if we're the least likely to be selected.

Benefit #7:
We Will Experience Preferential Treatment

You have already heard a number of my testimonies about the preferential treatment that I have received—treatment I neither asked for nor demanded. I've learned that if we come before God with a humble spirit, He will lift us up and give us preferential treatment.

James 4:10 says, "Humble yourselves in the sight of the Lord, and He will lift you up." Likewise, 1 Peter 5:6 instructs us, "Humble yourselves under the mighty hand of God, that He may exalt you in due time."

Centuries earlier, a young woman named Esther had experienced the kind of exaltation Peter wrote about:

> And Esther obtained favor in the sight of all who saw her. So Esther was taken to King Ahasuerus, into his

> royal palace, in the tenth month, which is the month of Tebeth, in the seventh year of his reign. The king loved Esther more than all the other women, and she obtained grace and favor in his sight more than all the virgins; so he set the royal crown upon her head and made her queen instead of Vashti. Then the king made a great feast, the Feast of Esther, for all his officials and servants; and he proclaimed a holiday in the provinces and gave gifts according to the generosity of a king (Esther 2:15-18).

Esther obtained favor and, as a result, was beloved by King Ahasuerus, who made her his queen. When the favor of God is on our lives, prominence and preferential treatment come right along with it.

WHEN THE FAVOR OF GOD IS ON OUR LIVES, PROMINENCE AND PREFERENTIAL TREATMENT COME RIGHT ALONG WITH IT.

Benefit #8:
Our Petitions Will Be Granted—Even by Ungodly Civil Authorities

We find more than one of the benefits of God's favor depicted in the story of Esther, the young Jewish girl who hid her identity and became queen of a vast area extending from India to Ethiopia. After learning of Haman's evil plot to kill all of the Jews in the kingdom, Esther formulated her own plan to petition the king for the lives of her people:

> At the banquet of wine the king said to Esther, "What is your petition? It shall be granted you. What is your request, up to half the kingdom? It shall be done!"
>
> Then Esther answered and said, "My petition and request is this: If I have found favor in the sight of the king, and if it pleases the king to grant my petition and fulfill my request, then let the king and Haman come to the banquet which I will prepare for them, and tomorrow I will do as the king has said." . . .
>
> So the king and Haman went to dine with Queen Esther (Esther 5:6-8; 7:1).

Although the king did not worship the God of the Jews—the God of Abraham, Isaac and Jacob—he granted Esther's petition because the favor of God rested upon her.

Benefit #9:
Policies, Rules and Law Will Be Changed or Reversed to Our Advantage

The decree calling for the death of all Jews had already gone forth, and the date had been set. Yet because of the favor of God that rested upon Esther, a new decree went forth:

> And the king held out the golden scepter toward Esther. So Esther arose and stood before the king, and said, "If it pleases the king, and if I have found favor in his sight and

> the thing seems right to the king and I am pleasing in his eyes, let it be written to revoke the letters devised by Haman, the son of Hammedatha the Agagite, which he wrote to annihilate the Jews who are in all the king's provinces. For how can I endure to see the evil that will come to my people? Or how can I endure to see the destruction of my countrymen?"
>
> Then King Ahasuerus said to Queen Esther and Mordecai the Jew, "Indeed, I have given Esther the house of Haman, and they have hanged him on the gallows because he tried to lay his hand on the Jews. You yourselves write a decree concerning the Jews, as you please, in the king's name, and seal it with the king's signet ring; for whatever is written in the king's name and sealed with the king's signet ring no one can revoke" (Esther 8:4-8).

Notice that not only did the king agree to set forth a new decree, but he also allowed Esther and her cousin, Mordecai, to write it as they pleased and then seal it with the king's own signet ring. The Bible goes on to say that "in every province and city, wherever the king's command and decree came, the Jews had joy and gladness, a feast and a holiday" (Esther 8:17).

Benefit #10:
We Won't Have to Fight Some Battles, Because God Will Fight Them for Us

Most of us are familiar with the words young David spoke to the Philistine giant before he killed him with a stone: "You come to me with a sword, with a spear, and with a javelin. But I come to you in the name of the LORD of hosts, the God of the armies of Israel. . . . Then all this assembly shall know that the LORD does not save with sword and spear; for the battle is the LORD's" (1 Sam. 17:45,47).

When we put our faith in God and His great favor, He will fight our battles for us. That's not to say we will never have to take a stand and exercise our faith, but we will certainly never have to fight our battles in our own strength.

> We have heard with our ears, O God, our fathers have told us, the deeds You did in their days, in days of old: You drove out the nations with Your hand, but them You planted; you afflicted the peoples, and cast them out. For they did not gain possession of the land by their own sword, nor did their own arm save them; but it was Your right hand, Your arm, and the light of Your countenance, because You favored them (Ps. 44:1-3).

One battle that God fought for Carolyn and me involved the changing of a law in Texas. Our two daughters were born 13 months apart, and when they were old enough to attend school, we anticipated that our younger daughter would start school one year behind her sister. However, because of her birth date, Texas law said that she would have to wait another year. Carolyn and I knew that she was capable of learning, and we didn't want her to be two years behind her sister.

We talked to the teacher, to the principal, and finally to the superintendent, who told us that although she understood our reasons for wanting the girls to be separated by only one grade, Texas law simply would not allow it.

So Carolyn and I decided to go over all of their heads, and we took our petition to God. We began to confess daily that the law would be changed in our favor—and by the time school started that year, the law had been rewritten, and our daughter was able to start school one year behind her sister. God fought our battle for us and even reversed the law to our benefit.

I'm telling you, walking in the favor of God has its benefits.

Putting a Demand on the Favor of God

We've just examined 10 specific benefits that come with walking in the favor of God. Although these benefits are ours to receive, they will not manifest in our lives if we don't put a demand on that favor. The way we put a demand on favor is by declaring it.

Looking again to Job 22:28, which we first examined in chapter 6, we read: "You will also declare a thing, and it will be established for you; so light will shine on your ways." The *Amplified* translation says, "And the light [of God's favor] shall shine upon your ways."

To declare means "to speak from the mouth." So according to Job 22:28, we will speak something and it will be established for us. Take salvation, for instance: We don't get to go to heaven until we open our mouths and lay claim to our salvation. The Bible says, "For with the heart one believes unto righteousness, and with the mouth confession is made unto salvation" (Rom. 10:10).

So in order to put a demand on the favor of God, we need to declare it. We need to get up in the morning declaring, "The favor of God goes before me today!" Throughout the day, whenever we think about it, we need to declare the favor of God—all the way up until we go to bed at night. If we make declaring the favor of God a natural part of our everyday lives, then we will see that favor manifesting in everything we do.

IF WE MAKE DECLARING THE FAVOR OF GOD A NATURAL PART OF OUR EVERYDAY LIVES, WE WILL SEE THAT FAVOR MANIFESTING IN EVERYTHING WE DO.

Personally, I don't leave my house without putting a demand on God's favor by declaring it. Doing so is as natural to me as putting on my clothes. I don't mean I declare God's favor every once in a while; I do it every single day of my life. And each time I see a manifestation of God's favor, I stop right then to acknowledge it and to thank Him for it.

Can you imagine what might happen over the course of one year if a person were diligent in declaring the favor of God? I'm not talking about just playing with putting a demand on God's favor to see if it will work. I'm talking about getting up every morning and declaring out loud the benefits that will come as a result of walking in God's favor. What do you suppose would happen if that person would not give up declaring favor, no matter how many attacks came against him or her? I am confident that in one year's time, that person would be able to look back and see manifestations of God's favor like never before.

Wise Solomon wrote that "a good name is to be chosen rather than great riches, [and] loving favor rather than silver and gold" (Prov. 22:1). In other words, favor produces things that money cannot buy. I've had this happen many times in my life, and I didn't have to spend one dime for what the favor of God produced. I've learned to confess for the favor of God instead of praying for money, because I know that favor will produce the kind of blessing that money cannot buy.

Psalm 5:12 says, "For You, O Lord, will bless the righteous; with favor You will surround him as with a shield." The human body naturally generates an electromagnetic field that can be detected with certain meters. I like to think of God's favor in a similar way: When God surrounds me with favor, there's a magnetic field of favor that follows me wherever I go. Anyone who comes into that sphere of influence is affected by what is on me. If I'm filled with joy, I can walk into a crowd of depressed people and my joy will affect them. When the favor of God is upon me and someone gets within my field, then God's favor is going to get on them, too.

I am happy to report that most of my staff members are prospering. They are blessed. They are experiencing favor like they've never known in their lives. Why? It's by association. They're associating with people who are blessed, who are prosperous, and who are experiencing the favor of God. The Bible says, "He who walks with wise men will be wise, but the companion of fools will be destroyed" (Prov. 13:20).

Translated literally from the Hebrew, Psalm 5:12 says that God will crown us with His favor. You can't see it, but I've got a crown of favor on my head at all times. It opens doors for me that no man can open, and it will do the same for you.

For reasons I will discuss in the next chapter, I believe that the Body of Christ has entered a season in which it is critical that we walk in the favor of God. I believe that those who are willing to put a demand on that favor by declaring it on a daily basis will see a substantial move of God in their lives.

Tremendous advancements will be made in the spirit realm during what I'm going to call this "season of favor." We will go further than we've ever gone, with more people experiencing prosperity and success than ever before—if they are willing to declare God's favor and then be quick to take hold of opportunities that are presented to them. In order to recognize and seize those opportunities when they come, we'll have to be sensitive to the Spirit of God. As a result of laying hold of these God-given opportunities, many believers will achieve financial independence and give more toward the work of the gospel than in times past.

I believe that during this season of favor, some will also experience more joy and happiness in their lives than ever before. My Bible says, "Happy are the people whose God is the LORD!" (Ps. 144:15). A lot of Christians are miserable, even though, according to the Word of God, they should be happy. Christians ought to be the happiest people on the planet, and I believe that we will be in this season of favor that is upon us.

Another thing that I believe will be manifesting to a greater degree in this season is divine direction. Some people will receive a clear sense of direction from the Lord—direction that will enable them to arrive, after many years of believing, at the places to which

God has been leading them. In some cases, this direction will have to do with changes they can make to positively affect their health. As a result of this direction, many will walk in a greater level of divine health, because they will put a demand on the favor of God.

During this present season of favor, many ministries will accomplish more in one year than they have previously accomplished in 10 years. This means that more souls will be won, and the harvest will be greater than what we've witnessed before. So don't give up on your loved ones; they're coming in. I don't care how far into sin the enemy has taken them—Jesus' love goes even farther, and He will bring them out.

DON'T GIVE UP ON YOUR LOVED ONES; THEY'RE COMING IN. I DON'T CARE HOW FAR INTO SIN THE ENEMY HAS TAKEN THEM—JESUS' LOVE GOES EVEN FARTHER, AND HE WILL BRING THEM OUT.

Now, just because we've entered a season of favor doesn't mean that everyone will experience it. Everything that happens to you will be directly connected to what you expect. When the apostle Paul wrote his letter to the Philippians, he was imprisoned and facing death. Yet he said, "For I know that this will turn out for my deliverance through your prayer and the supply of the Spirit of Jesus Christ, according to my earnest expectation" (Phil. 1:19-20). In other words, Paul was saying that he was going to get exactly what he expected.

No matter what comes your way during this present season of favor, expect the favor of God to go before you, expect the benefits of favor to manifest in your life, and expect God's favor to surround you.

If you do, you'll most certainly get exactly what you expect.

9

A DESIGNATED TIME OF FAVOR

As I've just described, I believe that the Church—meaning the Body of Christ—has entered a designated season of favor like no other generation has ever seen. I also believe that, according to the prophetic word of David found in Psalm 102, this season of favor will immediately precede the second coming of Jesus Christ.

> But thou, O LORD, shall endure forever; and thy remembrance unto all generations. Thou shalt arise, and have mercy upon Zion: for the time to favour her, yea, the set time, is come. For thy servants take pleasure in her stones, and favour the dust thereof. So the heathen shall fear the name of the LORD, and all the kings of the earth thy glory. When the LORD shall build up Zion, he shall appear in his glory (Ps. 102:12-16, *KJV*).

The term "Zion" is used more than 150 times in the Bible. In the Old Testament, Zion generally refers to the fortress of the city of Jerusalem, known also as the City of David. However, in the New Testament, Zion takes on an additional meaning that refers to God's spiritual kingdom–and, more specifically, to the Church. The apostle Paul, himself a Jew, understood this spiritual concept of Zion, saying, "You have come to Mount Zion and to the city of the living God, the heavenly Jerusalem . . . to the general assembly and church of the firstborn who are registered in heaven" (Heb. 12:22-23). So we see that Zion has both a literal and a spiritual meaning, each of which is indicated in David's psalm.

What many people fail to realize is that David was not only a psalmist, but also a prophet. He was a seer. He saw into the future. In fact, in Psalm 22, David saw more than a thousand years into the future and wrote about the crucifixion of the Lord Jesus. He even quoted the exact words Jesus would speak on the cross: "My God, My God, why have You forsaken Me?" (Ps. 22:1). On the day of Pentecost, Peter spoke the following words about David:

> Men and brethren, let me speak freely to you of the patriarch David, that he is both dead and buried, and his tomb is with us to this day. Therefore, being a prophet, and knowing that God has sworn with an oath to him that of the fruit of his body, according to the flesh, He would raise up the Christ to sit on the throne, he, foreseeing this, spoke concerning the resurrection of the Christ (Acts 2:29-31).

The reason I'm taking time to make this point about David is that we may see his reference to Zion in Psalm 102 not only in the literal sense, but also as a prophetic word about the Church.

In other words, David looked into the future and saw the set time of favor that was to come upon the Church.

To say there is a set time for something means that it is in the plan, in the mind, and in the will of God. It means nothing can change that which has been set. The word "set" is the same word you and I might use in referring to concrete. When a wet concrete mixture that has been poured into a form begins to dry, or set, it creates a solid foundation. It doesn't matter what happens to the structure built upon the foundation. The walls may come down, but the foundation is still set. Likewise, it doesn't matter whether someone believes it or not; God has a set time for His favor to be bestowed upon His Church, and nothing can stop that from happening.

Now let's see if we can pinpoint when this time might be. Verse 16 of Psalm 102 says, "When the LORD shall build up Zion, he shall appear in his glory" (*KJV*). Notice the reference to the appearance of the Lord Jesus Christ: "He shall appear in his glory." When? Although we don't know the day or the hour, we know it will happen at a time when God is building up Zion.

In Matthew 24, we find the account of Jesus talking to His disciples about the end of the age. When they asked Him, "Tell us, when will these things be? And what will be the sign of Your coming?" (Matt. 24:3), Jesus gave a detailed description of end-time events. He talked of wars and rumors of wars, famines, pestilences, earthquakes, false prophets and lawlessness, to name a few things (see Matt. 24:4-8). Certainly these signs have been experienced by virtually every subsequent generation to some degree, leading many to believe that the return of Jesus was imminent.

But until recently, there was always one piece of the puzzle that was missing.

As part of His response to His disciples' questions, Jesus said, "Now learn this parable from the fig tree: When its branch has already become tender and puts forth leaves, you know that summer is near. So you also, when you see all these things, know that it is near—at the doors! Assuredly, I say to you, this generation will by no means pass away till all these things take place" (Matt. 24:32-34). The fig tree Jesus spoke of is Israel, who put forth her leaves when she became a nation in 1948, thus providing God's "super sign" to the world that the coming of Christ is near. The missing piece of the puzzle has been set in place.

JESUS IS IN A BUILDING PROGRAM RIGHT NOW. NOT ONLY HAS HE BEEN BUILDING UP THE NATURAL ZION, BUT HE HAS ALSO BEEN BUILDING UP THE LOCAL CHURCH AND THE CHURCH UNIVERSAL.

You may not have realized this, but Jesus is in a building program right now. Not only has He been building up the natural Zion, but He has also been building up the local church and the Church universal—just as He promised to do when He said, "I will build My church, and the gates of Hades shall not prevail against it" (Matt. 16:18).

So both David and Jesus pinpointed a set time in which God's favor was to be poured out upon His Church, and that time is *now*.

I'm not saying that we haven't experienced the favor of God thus far. We have. In fact, the favor of God was manifest the day Jesus came to the earth as a babe. His birth was an expression—a manifestation—of the favor of God. Everything Jesus did during His earthly ministry was a manifestation of God's favor. His death and His resurrection were manifestations of favor. The facts that you and I have been made the righteousness of God and that we are new creations in Christ Jesus are manifestations of the favor of God.

Although you and I have had access to that favor since the day we made Jesus the Lord of our lives, I believe that what has come upon us now is a time of favor like no other generation has ever seen. In other words, I believe we are going to experience *exceeding* favor—a *beyond-the-norm* kind of favor—during this designated time. Paul talked about this kind of favor in his letter to the believers in Ephesus:

> And you He made alive, who were dead in trespasses and sins, in which you once walked according to the course of this world, according to the prince of the power of the air, the spirit who now works in the sons of disobedience, among whom also we all once conducted ourselves in the lusts of our flesh, fulfilling the desires of the flesh and of the mind, and were by nature children of wrath, just as the others.
>
> But God, who is rich in mercy, because of His great love with which He loved us, even when we were dead in trespasses, made us alive together with Christ (by grace

> [favor] you have been saved), and raised us up together, and made us sit together in the heavenly places in Christ Jesus, that in the ages to come He might show the exceeding riches of His grace [favor] in His kindness toward us in Christ Jesus (Eph. 2:1-7).

Notice that throughout most of this passage, Paul uses past-tense verbs, indicating that he's talking about things that have already taken place. But then, in verse 7, he refers to what will happen in the future: "that in the ages to come He might show the exceeding riches of His grace [favor] in His kindness toward us in Christ Jesus."

Paul started by describing things God had already done, but then he spoke about something that God was *going to do* in the ages to come. I would say that the ages to come that Paul wrote about are here today. In other words, we are in a designated time of favor in which we can expect God to show us His exceeding riches. This is God's set time to bring favor upon the Church, and this outpouring of favor will surpass anything the Church has experienced since its birth.

WE ARE IN A TIME OF FAVOR IN WHICH WE CAN EXPECT GOD TO SHOW US HIS EXCEEDING RICHES.

We read in the book of Acts that there was great favor on the Early Church. The Bible says that "continuing daily with one accord in the temple, and breaking bread from house to house, they ate their food with gladness and simplicity of heart, praising God and having favor with all the people. And the Lord added to the church daily those who were being saved" (Acts 2:46-47). God's favor upon the Early Church brought a great harvest of souls. I believe that harvest was also a shadow, or pattern, of the harvest we are going to experience in these last days.

Prophetic Patterns of Favor

As we study the Word of God, we find that God often did things in the Old Testament that were used as patterns for the pouring out of His favor as described in the New Testament. When God established an Old Testament pattern, He required mankind to carry out His detailed instructions with precision and accuracy.

For instance, when God established the Passover, which He instructed Israel to keep as a feast and an everlasting ordinance throughout all generations, the set time and method of sacrifice for the feast were specific. Throughout subsequent centuries and generations, each Israelite household sacrificed a male lamb at twilight on the set date, and then applied the blood of that lamb to the doorposts and lintel of the house. This pattern was rehearsed year after year until Jesus, who is the Lamb of God, was slain at the precise moment prescribed for God's Passover. Leaving no detail unfulfilled, God even saw to it that twilight's darkness covered the land for the three hours that Jesus was on the cross.

The Bible is full of Old Testament prophetic patterns that God established for His New Testament purposes. We find one of these patterns in the book of Isaiah:

> "Comfort, yes, comfort My people!" says your God. "Speak comfort to Jerusalem, and cry out to her, that her warfare is ended, that her iniquity is pardoned; for she has received from the LORD's hand double for all her sins." The voice of one crying in the wilderness: "Prepare the way of the LORD; make straight in the desert a highway for our God. Every valley shall be exalted and every mountain and hill brought low; the crooked places shall be made straight and the rough places smooth; the glory of the LORD shall be revealed, and all flesh shall see it together; for the mouth of the LORD has spoken" (Isa. 40:1-5).

Isaiah spoke of a designated time in which God would declare comfort, or favor, over His people. Then he uttered this familiar phrase: "the voice of one crying in the wilderness" (v. 3). These are the very words used by Matthew, Mark, Luke and John to describe John the Baptist.

In Psalm 102, David spoke of a time of favor, and here Isaiah referred to a time of comfort. The difference in the two prophecies is that Isaiah was seeing the first coming of Jesus, while David saw His second coming. For each of these events, God had already established an appointed time.

In Paul's letter to the churches in Galatia, he explained, "When the fullness of the time had come, God sent forth His Son" (Gal. 4:4). So as we read Isaiah's prophecies about the crucifixion, resurrection and substitutionary sacrifice of Jesus, we understand that he was seeing these events as they would happen at the appointed time. God would not allow Jesus to come any sooner than the appointed time. But once the prophecies of old had been fulfilled, and it was time for the Redeemer to manifest, nothing could stop His appearance.

Notice the pattern: Before Jesus came the first time, there was a manifestation of God's favor. When we hear about valleys being exalted, mountains being made low, and the crooked places being made straight, that's the favor of God in action. The favor of God was poured out before Jesus came the first time, and before He makes His next appearance, there will be a manifestation of God's favor like no generation has seen.

The *Amplified* translation of Ephesians 2:7 says that God will "clearly demonstrate through the ages to come the immeasurable (limitless, surpassing) riches of His free grace (His unmerited favor) in [His] kindness and goodness of heart toward us in Christ Jesus." Let's really take hold of the words "immeasurable," "limitless" and "surpassing." The word "surpassing" indicates a place we've never been before. "Immeasurable" and "limitless" imply that God's favor will manifest so often that we won't even be able to keep up with it.

I'm not saying that we won't be opposed, or that we won't experience some adversity. We will. But when the favor of God is on our side, we'll face adversity and overcome it just like the three Hebrew children did (see Dan. 3:19-30). They went through the flames and came out on the other side with not so much as a singed hair or the smell of smoke on their clothes. In so doing, they set an Old Testament pattern that will be fulfilled in and through us today.

Peter spoke of the fulfillment of another Old Testament prophetic pattern when he said, "But those things which God foretold by the mouth of all His prophets, that the Christ would suffer, He has thus fulfilled. Repent therefore and be converted, that your sins may be blotted out, so that times of refreshing may come from the presence of the Lord" (Acts 3:18-19). Peter was referring to the words the prophet Joel had spoken concerning God's refreshing of the land:

> Be glad then, you children of Zion, and rejoice in the LORD your God; for He has given you the former rain faithfully, and He will cause the rain to come down for you—the former rain, and the latter rain. . . . "So I will restore to you the years that the swarming locust has eaten, the crawling locust, the consuming locust, and the chewing locust. . . . And it shall come to pass afterward that I will pour out My Spirit on all flesh; your sons and your daughters shall prophesy, your old men shall dream dreams, your young men shall see visions. And also on My menservants and on My maidservants I will pour out My Spirit in those days" (Joel 2:23,25,28-29).

Joel saw into the spirit realm and described events that would not only take place in the land of Judah in his day, but also take place in the last days. We know that the last days began on the day of Pentecost, when God poured out His Spirit on 120 people who had gathered "to wait for the Promise of the Father" (Acts 1:4), as Jesus had instructed them to do. Many who observed the 120 that day thought they were drunk. But Peter explained, "These are not drunk, as you suppose, since it is only the third hour of the day. But this is what was spoken by the prophet Joel: 'And it shall come to pass in the last days, says God, that I will pour out of My Spirit on all flesh; your sons and your daughters shall prophesy'" (Acts 2:15-17).

Some Bible scholars describe the last days as a period of time lasting approximately 2,000 years. In that case, if the last days began on the day of Pentecost, then we must surely be near the end of the last days.

Looking again at Joel's prophecy, we see that there will be a restoration in the last days: God said He would restore the years that the locust had eaten. Peter affirmed this when he exhorted his listeners to repent, "that He may send Jesus Christ, who was preached to you before, whom heaven must receive until the times of restoration of all things, which God has spoken by the mouth of all His holy prophets since the world began" (Acts 3:20-21).

We can see from these Scripture passages that a major restoration is on God's agenda for the last days. I've been saying for many years that God is going to raise up an army that will literally march into the enemy's camp and take back everything that has been stolen from the Church. I believe we who are alive today are part of that army, and I believe we will fulfill the prophetic pattern of favor that was established when the children of Israel plundered the Egyptians as God delivered them out of 430 years of bondage.

Walking in Favor Takes Commitment

Just as Israel had to be committed to walking in the favor of God in order to break the bondage of slavery, we too must be committed to walking in the favor of God in order to live victoriously in these last days.

Some will take what they've learned about the favor of God and the importance of declaring it on a daily basis and approach it with the attitude: *Oh, isn't this wonderful! I think I'll try it.* Most people, when they say they are going to *try* something, are not yet committed. All it will take is a couple of trials, and they'll quit. If you're not committed, then declaring the favor of God on an occasional basis is not going to produce results.

I've had people tell me, "Brother Jerry, I heard what you said, and I tried declaring God's favor in my life, but it didn't work for me." My answer is always that being a *tryer* of the Word never produced results in anyone's life. It's the *doer* of the Word who is blessed:

> But be doers of the word, and not hearers only, deceiving yourselves. For if anyone is a hearer of the word and not a doer, he is like a man observing his natural face in a mirror; for he observes himself, goes away, and immediately forgets what kind of man he was. But he who looks into the perfect law of liberty and continues in it, and is not a forgetful hearer but a doer of the work, this one will be blessed in what he does (Jas. 1:22-25).

Simply put, where declaring the favor of God is concerned, to do nothing is to experience nothing.

Anytime we receive a revelation from God, He expects us to handle that revelation in a proper manner in order that we might be blessed. Moses established the prophetic pattern for handling that which God had spoken when he summarized the Law for a people who had already seen many of God's miraculous manifestations of favor.

> Therefore you shall lay up these words of mine in your heart and in your soul, and bind them as a sign on your hand, and they shall be as frontlets between your eyes. You shall teach them to your children, speaking of them when you sit in your house, when you walk by the way, when you lie down, and when you rise up. And you shall write them on the doorposts of your house and on your gates, that your days and the days of your children may be multiplied in the land of which the LORD swore to your fathers to give them (Deut. 11:18-21).

Moses told the people that not only should they lay up in their hearts and souls the things they'd learned, but also they should talk about those things day and night and teach them to their children. The promise attached to this command was that their days would be multiplied in the land. Where the favor of God is concerned, I do exactly as Moses instructed the Israelites to do. I declare God's favor consistently, on a daily basis. I talk to my wife about it, and we talk to our children and grandchildren about it. We talk to them about the designated time of favor that is upon us and about our expectations for greater manifestations of favor in our lives.

Earlier in this chapter, we read a passage from the book of Joel that talked about the former rain and the latter rain. The prophet Haggai offers this comparison: "The glory of this latter house shall be greater than of the former" (Hag. 2:9, *KJV*). I like to illustrate this promise by saying that the glory we see described in the Old Testament was just a moderate display compared to the glory that is to come.

THE GLORY WE SEE DESCRIBED IN THE OLD TESTAMENT WAS JUST A MODERATE DISPLAY COMPARED TO THE GLORY THAT IS TO COME.

When I look at the displays of God's glory and favor in the Old Testament, I personally think they are pretty awesome manifestations. But God calls them moderate. In essence, He is saying, "You haven't seen anything yet. If you think that was something, just wait until I turn up the volume."

Some people think it's strange to talk about God's plans for the future. But isn't that exactly what God does in His Word? If we're made in the image of God, shouldn't we be talking about His future plans as well? A vital part of my commitment to walking in the favor of God involves seeking the Lord as to what He plans to do so that I can be in the flow of it. After all, if you're in the know, you'll be in the flow.

God spoke through the prophet Isaiah, saying, "Behold, the former things have come to pass, and new things I declare; before they spring forth I tell you of them" (Isa. 42:9). As we read chapters 42 and 43 of Isaiah, it's clear that God is telling His people about the restoration He's about to bring into their lives. We also see that there is a problem. God can't get anybody to talk about what He is getting ready to do. "But this is a people robbed and plundered; all of them are snared in holes, and they are hidden in prison houses; they are for prey, and no one delivers; for plunder, and no one says, 'Restore!' " (Isa. 42:22).

What God is saying is this: "When I reveal to you what I want to do for you, I need you to start charging the atmosphere with My Word." The reason God wants us to charge the atmosphere with His Word is that the Word never returns to Him void. Isaiah 55:11 says, "So shall My word be that goes forth from My mouth; it shall not return to Me void, but it shall accomplish what I please, and it shall prosper in the thing for which I sent it."

The prophet Amos says, "Surely the Lord GOD does nothing, unless He reveals His secret to His servants the prophets" (Amos 3:7). Why would God first reveal to the prophets what He is preparing to do? Because prophets are not just seers; they also speak God's Word and His plans into the atmosphere. Jesus couldn't even come to earth in the flesh to redeem mankind until God had revealed His plan to the prophets and they began to speak it. This is how God births the supernatural into our natural environment.

God started speaking about Jesus' supernatural birth in the third chapter of Genesis, when He said to the serpent, "I will put enmity between you and the woman, and between your seed and her Seed; He shall bruise your head, and you shall bruise His heel" (Gen. 3:15). Throughout the Bible, children are never referred to as the seed of a woman. They are always spoken of as the seed of man—except in this reference. God was giving insight from the beginning that the One who would come to bruise the head of Satan would be a supernatural Seed coming through a supernatural occurrence that would take place at a designated time in the future. And so it happened:

> Now in the sixth month the angel Gabriel was sent by God to a city of Galilee named Nazareth, to a virgin betrothed to a man whose name was Joseph, of the house of David. The virgin's name was Mary. And having come in, the angel said to her, "Rejoice, highly favored one, the Lord is with you; blessed are you among women!"
>
> But when she saw him, she was troubled at his saying, and considered what manner of greeting this was. Then the angel said to her, "Do not be afraid, Mary, for you have found favor with God. And behold, you will conceive in your womb and bring forth a Son, and shall call His name JESUS." . . .
>
> Then Mary said to the angel, "How can this be, since I do not know a man?"
>
> And the angel answered and said to her, "The Holy Spirit will come upon you, and the power of the Highest will overshadow you; therefore, also, that Holy One who is to be born will be called the Son of God. . . . For with God nothing will be impossible."
>
> Then Mary said, "Behold the maidservant of the Lord! Let it be to me according to your word" (Luke 1:26-31, 34-35,37-38).

When Mary asked how this thing that Gabriel had just told her could possibly happen, she was thinking in the natural. The angel then explained that what God was about to do was not going to be brought about in the natural; it would be a supernatural occurrence. In order for this supernatural occurrence to take place, Mary had to become supernatural-minded. That's exactly what she did when she said, "Let it be to me according to your word." Her affirming words charged the atmosphere with faith for the supernatural.

I believe that, in this designated time of God's favor, there are many supernatural events and occurrences that God has prepared and made available for each and every believer who is willing to become supernatural-minded and charge the atmosphere with faith for miracles. But we will never be in a position to experience the supernatural if we're saying things like, "I tried confessing the favor of God in my life and it didn't work" or "Nothing like that ever happens to me." If we charge the atmosphere with negative words, we will have negative results.

We can't just talk any way we want and still expect God to pour out His supernatural favor in our lives. It isn't going to happen. First, we have to become supernatural-minded, and then we have to use our mouths to charge the atmosphere with faith.

The Bible says that "God . . . gives life to the dead and calls those things which do not exist as though they did" (Rom. 4:17). That's the way God operates. He calls things that do not exist as though they do.

In 2 Corinthians 4:13, we see that "since we have the same spirit of faith, according to what is written, 'I believed and therefore

I spoke,' we also believe and therefore speak." We have the same spirit as who? God. So if we have the same spirit of faith as God, then we're going to call things that do not exist as though they do.

Jesus said, "Out of the abundance of the heart the mouth speaks" (Matt. 12:34). When we become supernatural-minded, thoughts of the supernatural are going to get down into our hearts, and we won't have to *try* to charge the atmosphere with faith. It's going to spring out of our hearts and mouths all the time.

What you hear me say is what is in my heart in abundance. That's the reason you don't hear me talking about sickness and disease, failure and defeat. You don't hear me saying, "Woe is me" and "I don't know what we're going to do." This kind of thinking is not in my heart in abundance. Out of the abundance of my heart, my mouth speaks about the favor of God. My words then charge the atmosphere with faith for the supernatural to come to pass in my life.

Jesus said, "Have faith in God. For assuredly, I say to you, whoever says to this mountain, 'Be removed and be cast into the sea,' and does not doubt in his heart, but believes that those things he says will be done, he will have whatever he says. Therefore I say to you, whatever things you ask when you pray, believe that you receive them, and you will have them" (Mark 11:22-24).

I'm saying that I'm going to experience the fullness of the supernatural favor that God has designated for this time. Will you join me in saying it, too?

10

SUPERNATURAL FAVOR FOR OUR TIME

October 1970
Shreveport, Louisiana

On the final day of the conference at Carolyn's home church, the two of us were seated near the front of the auditorium, only steps away from Kenneth Copeland as he wrapped up his teaching from the fourth chapter of the book of Mark.

For the past four days, he had been using the parable of the sower to demonstrate the need for us to guard and nurture the Word of God that had been sown into our lives. "Satan comes immediately to steal the Word," he explained. "And anytime he attempts to do this, the circumstances he uses will most certainly test the quality of your faith."

As a young believer, I was taking everything Brother Copeland said to heart. Little did I know that the quality of my own faith would be tested within that very hour.

Parents have the innate ability to recognize the distinct cries of their own children. So when the nurse on duty for the childcare center rushed into the auditorium, carrying a screaming toddler, Carolyn and I knew instantly that it was our 13-month-old daughter, Terri. Even from a distance, we could see the huge bloodstain that covered the nurse's uniform, and as I took Terri into my arms, the source of the blood became apparent—it was coming from what was left of two of her fingers.

We found out that Terri had placed her hand beneath an occupied rocking chair, which had severed the ends of the two longest fingers on her left hand, just below her fingernails. Carolyn's and my faith was tested in that moment—and so was Kenneth Copeland's. I'll never forget what he did that day.

He stepped down off that platform, walked right up to me, laid his hands on Terri, and declared, "In the name of Jesus, I command this pain to stop and this bleeding to cease." Immediately, Terri stopped screaming, laid her head on my shoulder, and closed her eyes.

Then Brother Copeland looked me in the eye and said, "What do you believe?"

Without hesitation I told him, "I believe God will restore my baby's fingers."

"Good. I'm going to set myself in agreement with you and believe that these fingers will be restored. But you need to take her to the doctor so that she can be properly treated." With that he turned around, went back to the pulpit, and said to the crowd, "Now let's go back to Mark 4."

Before leaving for the hospital, we stopped in the restroom to wash Terri's bloody hand. That's where the nursery worker found us and handed me the two severed fingertips. Facing the stark reality of the situation, Carolyn and I knew we had a choice to make: We could respond to what we saw in fear, or we could respond in faith. We chose faith, and off we went to the hospital.

Dr. Simon Wall was one of the top plastic surgeons in Louisiana. After examining Terri that morning, he said, "I'm sorry, Mr. and Mrs. Savelle, but it is just not possible to reattach her fingertips. They are too severely damaged." With that, he took the two severed fingertips from my hand and discarded them.

He went on to explain that he would take a small graft of skin from Terri's hip and cover the ends of her fingers, but they would never be the same. "She'll never have fingernails, and the fingers will never be the right length. I'm sorry, but that's the way it is."

I said to him, "Sir, I'm not trying to be a smart aleck here, but I just want you to know that I do not accept what you say as final authority. The God I serve is a God who can restore."

"You don't understand, Mr. Savelle. What you are suggesting is medically impossible."

"I'll tell you what, doctor," I said. "You go ahead and do everything you can for her, and we'll believe that God will do the rest."

I was not suggesting that the doctor didn't know what he was talking about. He did know; he was at the top of his field. But at that time, I possessed something that T.L. Osborn describes as "young faith." This meant I had a faith that had not learned to doubt. So for the next six weeks, Carolyn and I stood firm in our faith, believing that God would restore our little daughter's fingers.

When we arrived at Dr. Wall's facility on the day the bandages were to be removed, it was apparent from a collection of statues displayed throughout his office that he served Buddha. Seeing those statues helped me to understand why the doctor was unable to believe that Terri's fingers could be restored. Neither medical science nor Buddha could do anything like that.

When Dr. Wall cut away the dressing from Terri's fingers, he raised his hands and yelled, "My God!"

I said, "What is it, doc?"

"Look," he said, holding up Terri's hand to show us her healed fingers, complete with perfect little fingernails.

I looked at the doctor and said, "No, sir, not *your* God. It's *my* God who did that, and His name is Jesus."

As it turned out, both Dr. Wall and his wife became Christians as a result of the miracle they witnessed when God restored our young daughter's fingers. Although I did not realize it at the time, God also used that experience to open my eyes to the real possibility of the supernatural favor of God manifesting in our lives on a regular basis.

Since my first experience with the supernatural more than 40 years ago, I've witnessed many such miracles and supernatural manifestations of God's favor—not only in my own life, but also in the lives of those to whom I've ministered. One time, I was preaching a sermon titled "Jesus the Oppression Breaker" to a large crowd in Nigeria. Pretty soon, I noticed people lifting wheelchairs and crutches high above the heads of those who had come to listen. Jesus was moving supernaturally among the crowd, healing those who had been unable to walk. That day, 21 others who had been blind from birth instantly received their sight.

Another time, during praise and worship at a conference in South Africa, the Lord spoke to me, saying, "I don't want you to preach your message tonight. Instead, I want you to continue in this flow of praise and worship. I'm going to do miracles in the midst of it."

When the meeting was turned over to me, I asked the worship team to continue ministering. I read aloud from Psalm 150, which talks about praising God with every kind of instrument. I had the pianist play, and then I directed the trumpet player to join in. Finally, I saw a guy standing by the bongo drums, and I told him to play. But he just looked at me and didn't move. So I said, "Do you hear me? I said praise God on those things." He went to the drums and started playing, and that's when the place erupted. What I didn't know was that the young man had never before played the bongos. But everyone else there knew it, and they understood the significance of what happened when the anointing of God came upon him to worship the Lord on the bongos.

As he played, and the worship team continued to minister, miracles started breaking out in the crowd of more than 8,000 people. One man, who was lying on a gurney near the door, had been brought to the meeting in an ambulance. Right in the middle of this time of praise and worship, he got off of the gurney and started running around the building, totally healed and set free. At another session in that same place, a woman's withered foot grew out right before our eyes, and we watched her walk around that building as normally as everyone else did.

In the four Gospels, we read numerous accounts of demon-possessed people being set free by Jesus. Although this isn't something we see on an everyday basis in the United States, it is not uncommon in other countries. A demon-possessed man was brought to an outdoor crusade I conducted in Kenya. Those who brought him had chained him to a tree in the open field where we were having the crusade, but I didn't know he was there.

At one point, I noticed a lot of noise and commotion coming from the direction of the tree, and I could see the crowd beginning to withdraw from that area. I left the platform to go see what was happening, and I was stunned to find this man chained to the tree, behaving like a wild animal. I walked up to him under the anointing of God and began to cast devils out of him, just like Jesus did in the Bible. It took a little while, but pretty soon, he was in his right mind. When they took the chain off of him, he lifted his hands and praised God.

Whether it's the restoration of a toddler's fingers or the healing of the sick or the deliverance of those who are bound by the devil, I've come to understand a powerful truth about the God we serve: He pours out His supernatural favor as an expression of His love for us—and as a demonstration of His love to unbelievers. Anytime there is a manifestation of this supernatural favor, lives are changed.

What Is the Supernatural?

We often associate the term "supernatural" with something that is weird. The supernatural is not weird, although Hollywood and the media would have us believe that it is.

Personally, I like Webster's definition: "departing from what is usual or normal [the norm] especially so as to appear to transcend the laws of nature." This definition takes the term "supernatural" out of the realm of the mystical and gives us something we can work with.

First, let's consider "the norm"; in particular, let's look at the present difficulties many people are having. For some, the norm may involve the loss of a job or a home. It may involve sickness or some form of bondage. In the natural, this is the way it is for many people. But it does not have to be this way for me or for you. I believe that in this designated season of God's favor, I am routinely going to experience the supernatural–a consistent departure from the norm.

Psalm 62:5 says, "My expectation is from Him." In other words, what we expect is what we get. It's a biblical principle–a spiritual law. If we expect the world's norm of loss, lack, sickness and bondage–or whatever the media tells us to expect–that's exactly what we will get. However, if we expect to see God at work in a situation according to His promises, that is what we will get. I like *THE MESSAGE* translation of this verse, which says, "Everything I hope for comes from Him."

We should never base our expectations on what the media says. In the book of Hebrews, the writer admonishes believers to lay aside all things that will ensnare and hinder them, and look unto Jesus (see Heb 12:1-2). The *Amplified Bible* says, "Looking away [from all that will distract] to Jesus" (Heb. 12:2). If we spend our time looking unto Jesus, we won't be hindered by distractions. But we can't focus on Jesus if we are at the same time paying attention to the media.

When we choose to look unto Jesus, we are actually positioning ourselves to experience the supernatural. Looking unto Jesus ensures that we will be in position to make a departure from the norm, which in turn positions us for lives of total victory. The Bible says that "God leads us from place to place in one perpetual victory parade" (2 Cor. 2:14, *THE MESSAGE*). This is the kind of life God wants us to experience.

The second part of Webster's definition of "supernatural" is "transcending the laws of nature." "Transcend" means "to rise above" or "to go beyond"; it doesn't mean "to do away with." For instance, whenever an airplane takes off, it transcends the law of gravity. The laws of lift, drag and thrust supersede the law of gravity, enabling the aircraft to take flight. All you have to do to find out if the law of gravity is still in place is turn the engines off. Likewise, I was not doing away with the laws of nature when I dared to believe that my daughter's fingers would be restored. I just had confidence in God's ability to supersede them.

THE SUPERNATURAL IS YOU AND ME DOING ALL WE'RE CAPABLE OF DOING IN THE NATURAL, AND THEN GOD STEPPING IN AND ADDING HIS "SUPER" TO IT.

As we can see, the supernatural is nothing more than a departure from the norm that comes through the transcending of the laws of the natural. Yet there is a part we have to play in seeing manifestations of the supernatural favor of God in our lives. I like to put it this way: The supernatural is you and me doing all we're capable of doing in the natural, and then God stepping in and adding His "super" to it.

This is exactly what happened when Jairus, a ruler of the synagogue, went to see Jesus about his dying daughter. Jairus said, "Come and lay Your hands on her, that she may be healed, and she will live" (Mark 5:23). But before Jesus could get to the child, a messenger came with word that she'd already died. As soon as Jesus heard this, He told Jairus, "Do not be afraid; only believe" (v. 36). Then Jesus went to Jairus's house and restored his little girl to life.

That healing was a manifestation of the supernatural favor of God, yet Jairus was required to do all that he could do in the natural before God added His "super" to it. The first thing Jairus did was to go to Jesus, which meant going against the grain of the norm of his day. Rulers of the synagogue were typically religious people who were not in favor of Jesus' ministry. So Jairus was actually laying his job on the line. The next thing Jairus did was to tell Jesus what he needed: "My little daughter lies at the point of death. Come and lay Your hands on her" (Mark 5:23). Finally, he continued to trust Jesus for the miracle his daughter needed even after receiving word of her death.

Jairus did his part; he took his expectation for his daughter's restoration as far as he could by going to Jesus, telling Him what he needed, and daring to believe what Jesus said in spite of a negative report. When Jesus saw that Jairus had done all he could do in the natural, He added His "super" to it, and the girl was raised from the dead. I'd call that a supernatural manifestation of God's favor!

It's important to note that in order to be positioned for the supernatural, we must be willing to do what Jesus tells us to do. When the rich young ruler came to Jesus and asked what he must do to inherit eternal life, Jesus told him to follow God's commandments. The young man said, "I have kept them from my youth." (As you may recall from our earlier discussion of this passage, the reason he was rich was that he'd obeyed the commandments throughout his life.)

We could say that this man came to Jesus thinking he'd done all he could do. But Jesus said, "You still lack one thing. Sell all that you have and distribute to the poor, and you will have treasure in heaven; and come, follow Me" (Luke 18:22). The Bible says the young man walked away sad and grieved at that saying. When Jesus revealed to him the one thing he wasn't doing, the man didn't want to do it. He wasn't willing to take his faith as far as he could in the natural.

The 10 lepers who saw Jesus from a distance were willing to take things as far as they could. Because they were considered unclean due to their leprosy, they were not allowed to enter the village. They would have been stoned had they done so. But they knew Jesus had the power and the authority to cleanse them from their leprosy, so they called out to Him, "Jesus, Master, have mercy on us!" (Luke 17:13).

Jesus said, "Go, show yourselves to the priests" (v. 14). The problem with what Jesus told them to do was that they *couldn't* go to the priests. They were unclean. The only time a leper could go to a priest was if the leper had been cleansed. Then the priest would declare him cleansed and welcome him back into the community.

So what was Jesus doing? He was speaking the end result. The 10 lepers obeyed Jesus, and the Bible tells us that they were cleansed as they went. They took their faith as far as they could in the natural; then God added His "super" to it.

If we want to see the supernatural favor of God manifest in our lives, we've got to be completely honest with ourselves, because the one thing we lack may be the one thing we do not want to hear.

IF WE WANT TO SEE THE SUPERNATURAL FAVOR OF GOD MANIFEST IN OUR LIVES, WE'VE GOT TO BE COMPLETELY HONEST WITH OURSELVES, BECAUSE THE ONE THING WE LACK MAY BE THE ONE THING WE DO NOT WANT TO HEAR.

We also need to quit giving God excuses as to what we can't do and what we don't have. When God called Moses to lead His people out of bondage in Egypt, Moses felt inadequate. In essence, he told God that the task was too big; he had nothing going for him other than a stick in his hand. But God told Moses He could use that stick if Moses would take the situation as far as he could in the natural—and we know that when God added His "super" to that natural stick, the supernatural favor of God manifested time and time again.

The supernatural favor of God will manifest in our lives, too, if we are willing to take our faith as far as we can in the natural.

We Are More than Conquerors

In his letter to the Romans, Paul asked, "Who shall separate us from the love of Christ? Shall tribulation, or distress, or persecution, or famine, or nakedness, or peril, or sword?" (Rom. 8:35). Paul then went on to say, "Yet in all these things we are more than conquerors through Him who loved us" (v. 37).

Without exception, Paul's generation and every generation since have experienced their share of tribulation. But as we discussed in the previous chapter, the events that we are experiencing in this present day meet the criteria for what Jesus described as the last days. When Jesus' disciples asked Him to show them the signs of the last days, Jesus talked about all kinds of calamities and chaos, such as wars, famines, pestilences and earthquakes in various places. He went on to say that there were two things believers must do to take their faith as far as they could in the natural:

> And Jesus answered and said to them: "Take heed that no one deceives you. For many will come in My name, saying, 'I am the Christ,' and will deceive many. And you will hear of wars and rumors of wars. See that you are not troubled; for all these things must come to pass, but the end is not yet" (Matt. 24:4-6).

In order to take our faith as far as we can in the natural, so that God can add His "super" to it, we must first "take heed that no one deceives [us]," and second, "see that [we] are not troubled." Jesus instructs believers to live in a troubled world without being troubled by it. How can we do this? How can we keep what is affecting the world from affecting us? By not being deceived. To avoid becoming deceived, we must refuse to allow the world's word to supersede God's Word.

When we say something like, "I know what the Word says, but . . ." we open the door to deception. "I know that the Bible says God will supply all my needs, but . . ." Get ready; you're about to be deceived.

If we want to prevent ourselves from being deceived, we must get to the place where the Word of God is the final authority in our lives. When I first received the revelation about the authority of God's Word more than 40 years ago, I didn't know where to begin. But I determined that I was going to make the Word of God the final authority in my life, no matter what the world said, no matter what my circumstances said, and no matter what some Christians might even have to say. When I stopped conforming to the world's norm, the troubles of the world had less and less effect on me, and the supernatural favor of God began manifesting in my life.

Jesus asserted that, in the last days, some terrible things would happen. All we have to do is watch the opening segment of a news report or pick up a newspaper to see that this world in which we live is indeed a troubled place. I am not denying that fact. I am not denying that you and I will come under attack or that we will have our challenges. I am not denying that we will from time to time experience the onslaughts of the enemy. What I *am* denying is the right of these troubles and attacks to affect me the way they affect those who are in the world.

Jesus said, "If the world hates you, you know that it hated Me before it hated you. If you were of the world, the world would love its own. Yet because you are not of the world, but I chose you out of the world, therefore the world hates you" (John 15:18-19).

To be "chosen" means to be "set apart"—but not necessarily removed. Notice that Jesus didn't ask His Father to take His disciples out of the world. Instead, He asked that they be kept from the evil one (see John 17:15).

TO BE "CHOSEN" MEANS TO BE "SET APART"—
BUT NOT NECESSARILY REMOVED.

We should not have an escape mentality that says, *Oh, God, take us out of this mess.* A supernatural mentality says, *I'm going to live right in the middle of this trouble and not be troubled by it.* We can do just that because we are in the designated season when the supernatural favor of God is being poured out in abundance.

When Jesus says that He has chosen us out of the world, another meaning of "chosen" is "to be made distinct." God has chosen us, set us apart, and made us distinct. I like to say that I'm a marked man. *THE MESSAGE* translation of Psalm 67:6-7 says, "You mark us with blessing, O God, our God." We are marked for blessing. We are not to be like the rest of the world. There's something distinctive about you and me, and that's because Jesus is our Lord. His supernatural favor and blessing on us separate us from the rest of the world.

When I read my Bible through from the beginning, I'm constantly amazed at how God has always wanted a people whom He could hold up to the rest of the world like a trophy and say, "Look at them. This is what happens when I'm your God." Israel is our biblical example of a distinctive people. God wanted other nations to look at the Israelites and say, "Their God is bigger and greater than our god."

God's plan has never changed. He is still looking for those whom He can hold up today, so He can say, "Look at the outpouring of supernatural favor that happens when I'm your God." But as I said before, in order for God to add His "super" to our natural, we must first take our faith as far as it can go.

The Bible says, "For indeed the gospel was preached to us as well as to them; but the word which they heard did not profit them, not being mixed with faith in those who heard it" (Heb. 4:2). This tells me that we can sit in the presence of the Word of God and hear the promises of God proclaimed, but—even though it is God's intent to fulfill those promises in the lives of every person who will believe them—there are some who will not see them fulfilled.

This doesn't mean that God is a respecter of persons, because the Bible makes it clear that He's not. It simply means that some people will take the Word of God and mix it with their faith, taking their faith as far as it will go in the natural, and others will not. If we want God to add His "super" to our natural, we have to take hold of His Word and become aggressive with it. We can't just hear it on Sunday and then not think about it again until the following Sunday. We have to confess God's Word every day of the week, and we have to confess God's favor every day of the week.

The devil is aggressive. He doesn't just attack on Sunday; he attacks 24/7. He's out to kill, steal and destroy. He doesn't want us to experience the supernatural favor of God. He wants us to suffer. He wants us to come up short. He wants us to experience lack, to be sick, and to lose our jobs and everything else we have. He's got one thing on his mind, and that's making our lives miserable. But we don't have to just sit back and take it.

First Peter 5:8 says that the devil comes "like a roaring lion, seeking whom he may devour." The Word doesn't say the devil *is* a lion; it just says he's trying to act like one. He *will* devour us—but only if we let him. If we understand our covenant with God and the authority we've been given over all the power of the enemy, instead of being devoured by trials, tribulations and troubles, we will have the supernatural favor of God to see us through them.

Peter said, "Beloved, do not think it strange concerning the fiery trial which is to try you, as though some strange thing happened to you; but rejoice" (1 Pet. 4:12-13). In other words, we shouldn't be shocked when we go through trials and tribulations. It's a part of life. Everybody experiences them. But notice that Peter says we are to rejoice. Why? Because we've come to understand and expect that we walk in a supernatural flow of the favor of God. And supernatural things happen when people *expect* the supernatural.

God is not holding anything back from us. He wants us to experience the supernatural, and He wants His Church to be the recipient of miracles in every encounter we have with Him. But we have to take our faith as far as it can go by *expecting* supernatural, miraculous encounters with God. So let's determine not to settle for anything less than God's best.

The time has come for us to move to a higher level of favor in God. I consider myself to have come a long way, but I know there is always a higher level to attain where God's favor is concerned.

Won't you join me now in answering His call to come up higher?

APPENDIX

TRUE STORIES OF THE FAVOR OF GOD

In this book, I have shared examples of how the favor of God has manifested in powerful ways in my life, and I hope that my stories will encourage you to seek God's favor for yourself. But I don't want you to rely on my testimony alone. During my years in ministry, I have had the privilege of speaking to countless brothers and sisters on this topic—and I have had the joy of seeing many of them apply the principles of God's favor with amazing results.

Here are just a few testimonies of how God has worked supernaturally in His children's lives as they have declared and depended on His favor in the face of different types of trials and needs. I have edited them from letters I have received over the years, but have kept them in first-person, as they are the stories of real people who have experienced the favor of God. As you read these accounts, I trust that you will be inspired to declare God's favor in your own life, and I look forward to someday hearing you share how He responded by exercising His abundant grace and favor in your behalf.

Favor in the Midst of Collapse

Since learning about the favor of God, my wife, Linda, and I have been experiencing the promise of Deuteronomy 28:2, which says, "All these blessings shall come upon you and overtake you, because you obey the voice of the LORD your God."

I can actually look back and take inventory of the occurrences of God's favor manifesting in many areas of our life. It has happened so many times that I now expect that favor to show up in my behalf.

Owning a real estate corporation in California has provided me with an excellent proving ground for a lifestyle of walking in faith. In a typical real estate transaction, there are many opportunities for problems to arise. I've found that difficulties often bring out either the worst or the best in those involved in the transaction, including buyers, sellers, lenders, agents, appraisers and inspectors. Regardless of the situation, I know that God is my source of supply, and that His favor surrounds me as a shield.

Before the housing market collapsed, our small firm was targeted by a worldwide real estate franchise whose profits were being impacted by our success. Not only did they court our employees, but they also threatened a lawsuit, claiming that the color we used on a portion of our yard sign violated their copyrighted signs. The favor of God delivered us from that situation, and the company that had come against us ended up closing their office in our area.

In 2006, we opened a second office, and the favor of God not only brought us $45,000 worth of new office furniture and equipment, but also enabled us to move in with very little start-up cost. When the market collapsed, and many of our agents had to find employment outside the real estate industry, we decided to close that office. But God's favor provided us with a tenant that took over the lease and even paid us a commission for our services.

Prior to the collapse of the real estate market, I had negotiated to represent the developer of a housing tract slated to contain 28 homes, some of which were already under construction. When the market collapsed, the builder lost his funding, leaving 12 empty houses and an unfinished tract of land. For the next two years, I regularly drove through that tract, confessing that the favor of God would enable me to sell those homes. One day, I got a call from a construction company that had purchased the site and was going to complete the homes. A broker whom I had never met had given the new owners my name and told them to call me because I was a nice guy. The favor of God overtook me and made it possible for me to list and sell all 12 of the finished homes.

We have experienced God's favor in receiving many listings from REO banks, and we have assisted countless buyers to secure homes. Every car we have owned since we first began to declare the favor of God has been paid off in less than a year. Our business remains profitable, and we have been able to help our children with their college and living expenses. The favor of God has given us vacations, parking spots, shopping deals and hotel rooms. In every type of situation, God always finds a way to make sure we are favored.

After having experienced the favor of God and an unending source of supply for so many years, Linda and I heard the Lord speak in 2010, saying that we needed to finish our commitments, sell our home, and be willing to move as He would direct us into ministry. We have been blessed to live in one of the nicest homes in our area, but the Lord told us that He has prepared a home that is much better for us. Although He said that we would not be able to understand until we see it, I believe Him, because He always favors us. As we prepare for the move, I declare daily that we will leave this place the same way the children of Israel left Egypt—with gold in our pockets.

I do not always know when, where or how it will happen, but the favor of God always shows up to bless me, my family, our business and our ministry. —**Bill and Linda Sue**

A Home of Their Own

For most of our married life, my wife and I have rented a house. We went through a bad buying-selling experience early in our marriage, and we did not want to go through that again. But as we started to learn about the favor of God, we realized that to experience God's best, we needed to find out His will for us in various situations. So, we determined to do this in regard to owning a house.

After a season of listening to God, we began to feel that we should move to the Fort Worth, Texas, area. We spent many Sunday afternoons driving around Fort Worth, declaring the favor of God as we searched for just the right house. Two Scripture verses spoke powerfully to us during this time: "And I will provide a place for my people . . . so that they can have a home of their own"

(2 Sam. 7:10, *NIV*), and "GOD himself will build you a house!" (2 Sam. 7:11, *THE MESSAGE*).

One Sunday evening, as we were driving past the community of Stephenville, located just southeast of Fort Worth, its lights seemed to beckon to us. We turned to each other and said, "This is home!" We realized that although we had been searching for a home in the right general area, we had not been looking in quite the right place. Stephenville was where God wanted us to be, and we believed that His favor would lead us to the right house there.

God confirmed His direction a short time later, when we ran into two friends at a restaurant where we were dining. One was a realtor who said that he'd just told his wife, "I need to get Jim and Margie a house." Imagine his surprise when we told him that we agreed with him. We found favor with our bank, and we were quickly pre-approved for a loan. Now we just had to find our new home.

We looked at house after house, but none of them seemed just right. When we found one that we thought we could make do, we put in an offer. But it already had an offer pending, so we kept looking. We found a neighborhood that we really liked, but we felt certain that the houses were out of our price range. To our surprise, our realtor told us that the properties in this neighborhood were in fact within our range, and we found one on a corner lot that really appealed to us. Unfortunately, it had a "sale pending" sign in the front yard.

We were becoming discouraged, yet we kept declaring the favor of God where our new house was concerned. One day, as we were driving around the neighborhood, collecting sales brochures, we noticed that the "sale pending" sign on the corner house was gone, and a "for sale" sign was up in its place. We contacted our agent and made an appointment to see the house that same day. Our realtor told us that the potential purchaser's loan had fallen through only that morning. The minute we stepped inside that house, we knew that it was home. We wrote an offer, which was accepted immediately, and six weeks later we closed on our new house. God not only provided the down payment and closing costs, but He also provided money to buy new furniture for the house, which was twice the size of our rental.

When a friend came to visit us in our new home for the first time, she said, "I need to tell you one thing about your new house. I saw the one you moved from, and I know that most people would go one step up in size from that house, and then in time would take another step up into a house like this. But the two of you have gone from there to here in just one step."

Margie turned to her and said, "That is the favor of God; we are blessed with His favor." Other friends have also seen the favor of God upon our lives. Some do not know what it is, but we do—and we give Him all the glory and praise. As the prophet Isaiah writes, "All who see them [in their prosperity] will recognize and acknowledge that they are the people whom the Lord has blessed" (Isa. 61:9, *AMP*). —Jim and Margie

God's Handiwork

My wife, Deborah, and I were living in the concrete jungle of downtown Chicago, working long hours completing projects for advertising clients. Being able to take time away from work to look at what God has made has always been an important respite for us. That particular year, we visited the islands of St. Thomas and St. John, where we spent time relaxing, being with God, and enjoying each other. As we took a boat from one island to the other, I was so overwhelmed by the beauty of the area that I cried as I soaked in God's handiwork.

That vacation in the islands led us to believe God for a home there. In fact, a couple of years later, when we were wandering around the seacoast, we found the perfect house in the perfect location–right on a little beach on the island of St. John. We soon found out that the National Park Service owned the house, but we were bold in faith and claimed that it would one day be ours. We knew that the favor of God could overcome anything, even the government, to get us our dream house.

Walking with the Lord is always a learning experience, if we are open to His wisdom and leading. After believing for two years that the house on St. John would one day be ours, we heard the Lord speak to us, asking us to release the house. To be honest, at first we were somewhat let down, but then we remembered something we had learned about God's favor: If God asks you to give something up, He has something better for you. So we released the claim of faith we had placed on the house.

As we traveled to the islands on a frequent basis, we realized that it would actually be more practical to have a house on St. Thomas, where the airport was located, and where there was access to grocery stores and other necessities. So we put our faith in God to provide a beach house for us on St. Thomas. We were told that this was impossible, because the best beach properties belonged to the resorts, and there was no private property available.

For two more years, we continued to believe that the favor of God would provide us with a beach house. Then we met a realtor, a man in his sixties with sparkling eyes, who knew everyone on the island. He said to give him a week, and he would show us exactly what we wanted.

As it turned out, at the same time that we had released the beach house on St. John two years earlier, a wealthy landowner with holdings all over the islands made an important decision. He relinquished a 50-acre parcel of land, which he had originally reserved for his family, to be developed. Because God had moved on this man's heart to change his plans, we had the opportunity to purchase an acre of beachfront property, where we then built the exact house we had always wanted. Without the favor of God operating in our lives, this never would have happened. —Richard and Deborah

Moving a Mountain of Debt

In December 2011, the Lord spoke to me about 2012, saying that it would be not only my year of prosperity, promotion and increase (financially and spiritually), but also a year of answered prayers, turnaround and "suddenlies." Around that same time, I heard teaching about the favor of God that confirmed what God was telling me.

As the new year approached, I began decreeing out loud God's favor and blessing over myself every day before leaving my house.

One day, I checked one of my credit card balances to see how much I needed to pay, and to my surprise the amount was significantly lower than what I expected. When I saw the entry that said "merchandise finance refund: $725.90," I had to leave my desk at work and run to the restroom, where I could shout and thank God for His favor in my life.

I believe that this blessing is just the first of many manifestations that are coming my way not only in 2012, but also in the following years. I have determined to walk by faith, to stand on the Word of God, and to dare to believe God.

I am expecting to be debt-free in 2012, and I believe that my God is well able to do that for me. —Yvonee

A Shadow of Things to Come

Since I first learned about the favor of God, I have seen numerous instances of God's favor manifesting in my life. One of my favorite examples involves a pair of motorcycles.

I had purchased a Honda Shadow from a young man who was selling it to meet a financial need. After I had owned the bike for almost a year, God spoke to me about sowing it into the life of someone who needed it. But before I did that, He wanted me to look for the exact bike I would like to have.

At the Harley-Davidson store, I found and fell in love with a Harley 100th Anniversary Edition. I asked the salesman to write all of the specifications on a sheet of paper, which I then placed in my Bible beside the page that says, "And the Lord answered me and said, Write the vision and engrave it so plainly upon tablets that everyone who passes may [be able to] read [it easily and quickly] as he hastens by" (Hab. 2:2, *AMP*).

Two months later, just one week before Jerry Savelle's motorcycle rally in Granbury, Texas, I gave the Honda Shadow to someone who really needed it. On the day of the rally, I returned to the Harley store and looked at my dream bike again. While I was there, a friend called and asked what I was doing. I told her I was at the Harley store, looking at bikes, and she said, "Wait right there. I'm on my way." I thought that she needed to talk to me, or perhaps she needed prayer.

My friend arrived a short time later, stunning me when she said, "The Lord told me to buy you a Harley today." Pointing to the bike I had been looking at, she asked, "Is that it right there?" When I said yes, she told the salesman that we would take it, and then she said she also wanted to purchase the best warranty. As she was writing out the check, the salesman asked for her name so he could put it on the title. She said, "This is Ken's bike. I'm just doing what God told me to do, so put the title in his name." Then she turned to me and said, "Well, I've obeyed God, so now you go to Brother Savelle's motorcycle rally." Then she got in her car and drove off.

I was humbled and thankful for the favor of God working in my life that day. God has used that motorcycle (and the story about how I got it) to manifest His favor in the lives of other people as well—people whom I have led to Christ or whose faith has increased after hearing my testimony. Actor Gary Busey once commented that someone should make a movie about my life, and I'm believing that one day many more people will know how the favor of God has affected my life on a daily basis.

To God be the honor and glory for His favor! —Ken

Roadside Assistance

One evening, my car stalled suddenly while I was driving home; apparently the battery was dead. I had a huge presentation to make at school the next day, I was involved in a legal dispute, and I was already tired and overwhelmed with so much pressure. Now this.

I had been listening to a message about God's favor and had been confessing His favor over and over again. When I called my car insurance company, they offered to tow my car at no charge. The tow truck arrived in less than 30 minutes and took my car to the dealership.

I found out that the car needed several repairs, including an $800 alternator (not covered by warranty). The total bill was going to be more than $1,000, which represented half of my savings. I told the service representative I would call him back shortly to give him the okay to proceed, but about 10 minutes later, he called me again. He said, "We don't usually do this, but we will pay for the alternator because we appreciate you as a customer."

As I yelled, "Thank You, Jesus!" into the mouthpiece of the phone, I thought to myself, *That's the favor of God!* The repair bill was reduced to an amount that I was comfortable with, and I'm now sowing and believing that my savings will be restored completely. —Cyntillia

A Building for a Buck

When my wife, Iliana, and I started our church, West Coast Believers Center International (WCBC), we made a conscious decision to depend upon the favor of God to cover our ministry. As we moved forward in obedience, our congregation immediately began to experience tremendous miracles of God's favor.

At our very first service, we were given a brand-new sound system, complete with speakers, a 24-channel soundboard, cables, microphones and a wireless lapel microphone. During our first year of ministry, we experienced supernatural debt cancellation and supernatural increase of our resources. Our first utility bills showed credits. It wasn't just the church that experienced this favor; the people who helped us to plant WCBC did, too. One man's home electric bill consistently read $1.35 for an entire year. When he had the electric company check the meter, the technician said, "We can't find anything wrong with your meter, sir."

The greatest manifestations of God's favor happened right before our first anniversary. The Lord told us that April of that year would be a resurrection month for the ministry, and that the people who were attending the church at that time needed to be ready for it. He said that He would be sending us more people. We had not experienced any marked growth during our first year, but that April we had 50 visitors in one service alone, and within three months our congregation had grown to more than 200 people.

Shortly thereafter, another local congregation whose pastor had moved away approached us. They said they had heard good things about us and asked if we would consider merging the two churches, joining them at their location. We prayed and felt that this opportunity was of the Lord—and within one month, two good churches became one great church.

Two weeks later, we received word that the building the church was leasing had been sold. My first action as pastor of our merged congregation was to meet with the building's new owners to discuss the possibility of renewing our lease, which was set to expire in four months. We began to pray for the favor of God to go before us and touch the hearts of those with whom I would speak. I felt the favor of God so strongly that I began to confess that we would be allowed to remain in the building at a cost of $1.00 for an entire year. Some people laughed, and others thought I was crazy, but none of these things moved me.

When the day came for me to meet with the president and board members of the organization that had purchased the building, I told them about the ministry, our vision, and the things that we had already accomplished. When all was said and done, the president turned to me and said, "Pastor Bulger, we like you, and we like the things that you are doing for the community. So here's what we're going to do: Your lease expires in four months, but we are going to extend the lease for one year for a total annual cost of only $1.00." *Praise God for His favor!*

We needed that building more than we needed money for the rent, and God's favor gave us both. During the year we were in that facility, we began holding double services, and when our 12 months were up, we had outgrown the building. The favor of God gave us that first building, and it has given us every building we have occupied since then.

The Word of God and our experience as a church have taught us that when we think we need to be praying for finances, what we really need is the favor of God—because the favor of God can do more than what money can buy. —Dr. Joshua and Iliana

To Catch a Motorcycle Thief

One time we saw favor was in the early 1990s. I went with a group of students and a few other guys to Daytona Bike Week, which is one of the largest gatherings of bikers in the country. I rode down on my favorite Harley. While we were there, I let one of the friends who had come down with us borrow my bike, and I used another one.

At these kinds of events, there are thousands of bikes, and there are also groups of thieves that ride around in vans, looking for people who don't lock up their motorcycles. They take the unlocked bikes and put them in the van. Then the van goes up the interstate about 60 or 70 miles, to a spot where there is a big tractor trailer waiting. They load the bikes into it, take them apart, and sell the parts at swap meets. Sometimes they'll take a bike up north, put new VIN numbers on the frame and engine, and either use it themselves or sell it up there. Generally, once the bike is taken, it's gone, and you don't ever hear about it again.

Well, we went in to eat dinner one night, and those people rolled up in a van while we were eating and not paying attention. Too Tall, the guy I had let borrow my bike, hadn't locked it, and it got stolen while we were inside.

We came back to Alabama, where we lived, and I pretty well knew what had happened to that bike. Anyone else who knew anything about the biker world knew what had happened to it, too, and was laughing, saying, "That bike is gone forever." But then . . . the favor of God entered the picture.

When you know that God loves you, and you have found His favor by serving Him with all your heart, amazing things happen. Eight months after our trip, I got a call from a detective down in Daytona Beach, Florida. He asked if I owned such and such a motorcycle and had reported it stolen eight months earlier.

I told him, "Yes, sir."

He said, “Well, we have your motorcycle.” My jaw dropped open, and you can imagine the surprise on my face. I realized that the favor of God had once again come in my life in a huge way.

The detective said they had pulled over a man riding my bike out on the interstate. Florida is a helmet law state, and he wasn’t wearing a helmet. When they pulled him over and went through the motorcycle, they found a helmet in the saddle bag. Because he wasn’t wearing it, they ran the VIN number, and it matched my bike.

The detective told me I was free to come get it anytime I wanted to. So I went back to Daytona Beach with my son, Joshua, and a student we called “Bull,” and sure enough, there was my motorcycle—my Harley Davidson, one of my favorite bikes in the entire world—and it was basically untouched. The guy had left it sitting outside, and some rust was getting on it, but it didn’t take much to knock the rust off—and then there it was, good as new. Once again, the favor of God showed up and showed out in my life. —Mac

Let the Champion in you ARISE!

Called to Battle Destined to Win
Jerry Savelle
ISBN 978.08307.51297
ISBN 08307.51297

When tough times come, what do you do? Complain? Throw in the towel? Head home? If you are like most people, you give up. But God wants you to stay in the battle and prevail over whatever difficulties you are facing. God has chosen you to fight this battle, and He has given you a destiny to experience His breakthrough power. What's more, He will provide everything you need to pursue, overtake and recover what has been lost. Jerry Savelle has been in the battle and emerged to tell about it. Through enthralling stories, solid teaching and inspired motivation, he will show you how to persevere when situations are tough and stand on the Word of God until victory is achieved. The pain, disappointments or failures in your past cannot overcome God's purposes for your life when you trust His promise that He will always show up when you refuse to back down. So let the hand of God work in and through you to say no to giving up and yes to becoming a champion!

Available at Bookstores Everywhere!

Go to **www.regalbooks.com** to learn more about your favorite Regal books and authors. Visit us online today!

www.regalbooks.com